Robert H. Goddard

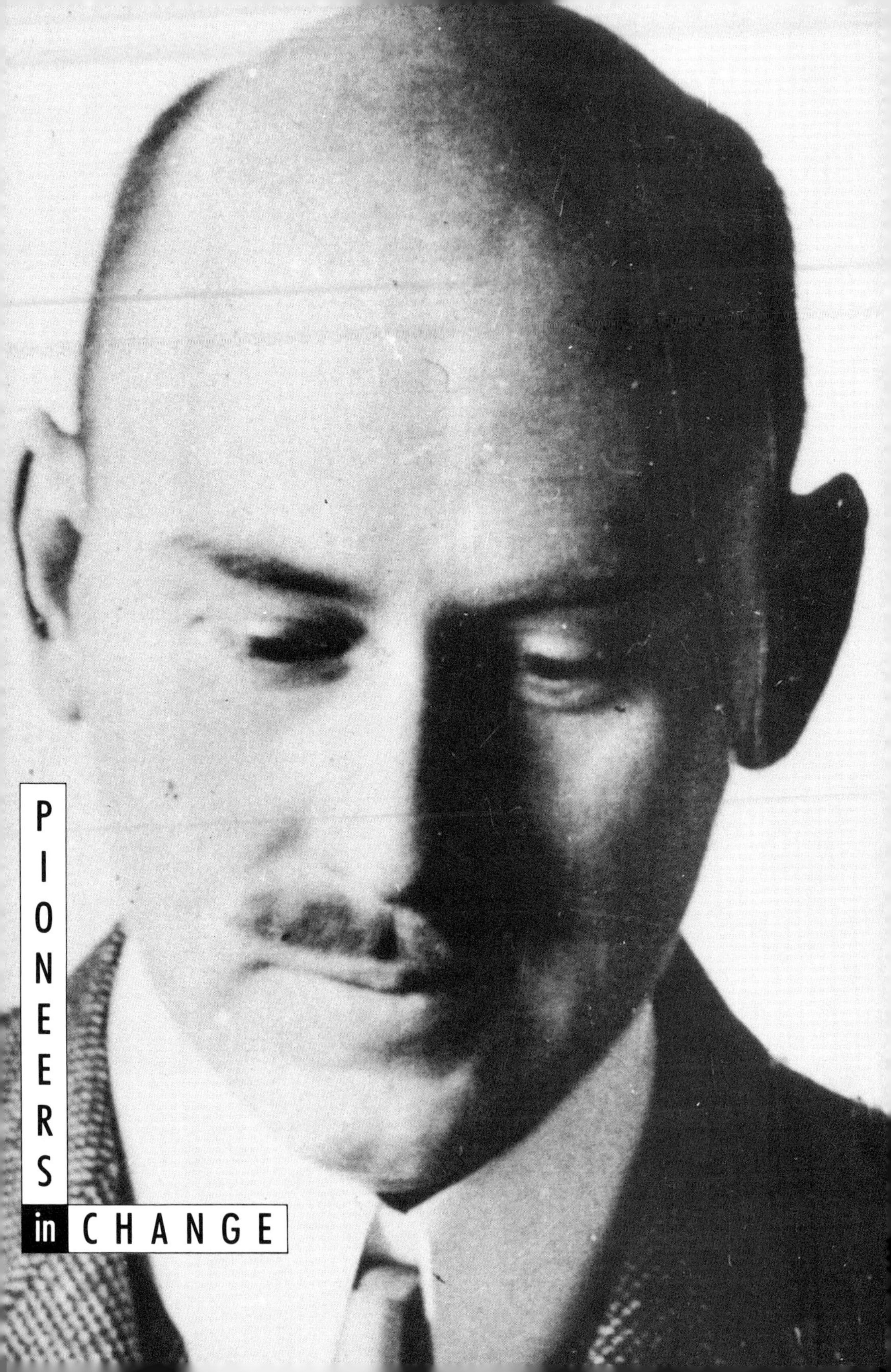
PIONEERS
in CHANGE

Robert H. Goddard

KARIN CLAFFORD FARLEY

Silver Bu

To Jack

CONSULTANTS:

Robert M. Goldberg
Consultant to the Social Studies Department
  (former Department Chair)
Oceanside Middle School
Oceanside, New York

Michael Kort
Associate Professor of Social Science
Boston University

TEXT CREDITS:

© Copyrighted, Chicago Tribune Company, all rights reserved, used with permission.

The First Hundred Years at the Smithsonian Institution 1846–1946, by Webster P. True, Washington, D.C.: Smithsonian Institution, 1946.

LIFE SCIENCE LIBRARY: *Man and Space,* by Arthur C. Clarke and the Editors of Time-Life Books, © 1975 Time-Life Books Inc.

A Method of Reaching Extreme Altitudes, by Robert H. Goddard, Washington, D.C.: Smithsonian Institution, 1920.

The Papers of Robert H. Goddard, Volumes 1, 2, 3 (New York: McGraw-Hill, 1970), Esther C. Goddard and G. Edward Pendray, editors. Robert Hutchings Goddard Library, Clark University/Goddard Collection/Archives.

Reprinted with permission of the Worcester Telegram & Gazette.

PHOTOGRAPH ACKNOWLEDGMENTS:
Courtesy of Farrar, Straus & Giroux: p. 119; Goddard Collection/Clark University: pp. ii, 5, 9, 13, 27, 39, 49, 56, 58, 89, 93, 95, 100, 123, 129; Courtesy of HarpersCollins Publisher: p. 62; UPI/Bettmann: p. 118; Courtesy U.S. Patents Office: p. 29.

SERIES AND COVER DESIGN:
R STUDIO T Raúl Rodríguez and Rebecca Tachna

PHOTO RESEARCH:
Omni-Photo Communications, Inc.

Published by Silver Burdett Press, Inc., a division of Simon & Schuster, Inc., Englewood Cliffs, NJ 07632.

Library of Congress Cataloging-in-Publication Data

Farley, Karin
  Robert Goddard / Karin Clafford Farley
    p. cm.—(Pioneers in change)
  Includes bibliographic references and index.
Summary: A biography of the scientist who developed the first liquid propelled rocket.
  1. Goddard, Robert Hutchings, 1882–1945—Juvenile literature.
  2. Rocketry—United States—Biography—Juvenile literature.
[1. Goddard, Robert Hutchings, 1882–1945. 2. Scientists. 3. Rocketry.] I. Title. II. Series.
        TL781.85.G6R63   1991
        829.4'092—dc20
            [B]   90-26706
                                                                      CIP
                                                                       AC

Manufactured in the United States of America.
ISBN 0-382-24171-1 [lib. bdg.]
10 9 8 7 6 5 4 3 2 1
ISBN 0-382-24177-0 [pbk.]
10 9 8 7 6 5 4 3 2 1

CONTENTS

1

Martians

After the Civil War came the revolution—the Industrial Revolution. It transformed the way of life in the United States.

Before the Civil War started in 1861, most people worked at farming. They raised their own food, wove their own cloth, created their own furniture, and forged their own tools. They even made their own light—candles. All these family products were produced with simple hand tools. Even such things as guns and silverware were crafted by workers in their own small shops attached to their homes.

Not until after the Civil War were machines powerful enough and cheap enough for widespread use. Industry was taken out of homes and small workshops and put into large factories.

People were fascinated by what machines could do for them. There was an explosion of a new phenomenon—

modern technology. This use of science to achieve practical purposes spurred the interest and imagination of inventors and scientists. In 1837, Samuel F. B. Morse invented a working model of the telegraph, and the first telegraph message was sent between cities in 1844. Two years later Elias Howe invented the sewing machine. In 1876, Alexander Graham Bell sent the first voice message over his invention, the telephone. Thomas Edison developed the first practical electric light bulb in 1879. In 1895, Guglielmo Marconi in Italy sent the first wireless telegraph message by electrical waves through the air. This led to the invention of the radio and mass communication. The Wright brothers made the first power-driven, heavier-than-air machine fly in 1903. Although it flew only 120 feet in twelve seconds, the age of the airplane had begun.

Massachusetts had been in the forefront of the Industrial Revolution with heavy industry all over the state. Textile mills thrived in Lawrence, Pittsfield, and Fall River. Lowell was famous for its cotton mills. Shoes were mass-produced at Lynn and Weymouth. The city of Worcester was considered Massachusetts's industrial heart. In this town in the middle of the technological wonder years, Robert Hutchings Goddard was born on October 5, 1882.

His father was Nahum Danford Goddard, a bookkeeper for the L. Hardy Company, which made cutting tools for industry. Young Nahum had fallen in love with the boss's daughter, seventeen-year-old Fannie Louise Hoyt. When Nahum and Fannie were married on January 3, 1882, her father so strongly objected that he disinherited her. But Fannie was warmly welcomed into the Goddard family home, Maple Hill. Her mother-in-law, Mary Pease Upham Goddard, was delighted to have a daughter, at last. Madam Goddard, as she was called, dearly loved her grandson, born in October 1882. She took over the care of the baby from her young and fragile daughter-in-law.

Whether it was to escape his disapproving father-in-law or his take-charge mother, Nahum Goddard quit his job the next year and moved with Fannie and their baby to Roxbury. In this suburb of Boston, he settled them into a frame house with a large backyard on Forest Street. He found another job in a small factory that produced knives. But he felt it was important to work for himself instead of for others. With a partner, he soon purchased the business and renamed the company Stubbs and Goddard.

Nahum Goddard loved the age he lived in. He was fascinated by the new inventions that seemed to come along every year. In his home, he installed electric lights and Thomas Edison's new contraption, the wonderful phonograph. He was an early owner of a radio and an automobile. Nahum Goddard was an inventor himself. He devised a new type of knife for machines that cut rabbit fur, used in making hats. Another invention was a type of flux, a substance used to fuse or weld together metals. It was called the Goddard welder.

Nahum Goddard shared his enthusiasms with his little son. He took Robbie, as he was called, for rides on Boston's new underground trolley, which soon was called the subway. He patiently explained the new machines on a level the child could understand.

Robbie was especially interested in electricity. He said once, "Electricity appealed to me as something bordering on the supernatural." By the age of four or five, Robbie was fascinated by the sparks he created by scuffing his little shoes across a carpet and by the sparks produced by a dry-cell battery. One day, he took a battery apart. Holding the zinc from the battery in his hand, he scuffed his shoes along a gravel walk. Then he climbed a low fence and jumped off, thinking the electricity on his shoes and the zinc rod would make him fly. His mother's good-natured warning that he might jump so high he could fly off and never come back convinced the toddler scientist not to do that experiment again.

Robbie went to Mount Pleasant Primary School and O'Brien Elementary School. One of his worst subjects was arithmetic. He understood it, but he kept coming up with the wrong answers and getting poor grades. One day, all his friends were taking the entrance tests for Roxbury Latin School, a private school. Robbie didn't plan to go there, but he took the tests because he didn't have anything better to do. Imagine his great surprise when he scored the highest grades of anyone in mental and written arithmetic. He had always considered himself a below-average student.

In some ways, Robbie took after his grandfather Nahum Parks Goddard, a professional violinist. Robbie played the piano and sang in the choir of St. Anne's Church. One year the church put on a pageant called "A Sixteenth-Century Christmas." As part of the chorus off-stage, Robbie was to be heard and not seen. The boys found the long waits between singing their songs boring and began goofing off. Robbie fell down a flight of stairs into the basement and was briefly knocked out. He came to as he was being carried out of the dark by someone dressed in a red devil's costume. It gave him a fright for a few minutes to think he had "passed on" and gone to hell.

On summer vacations from school, Robbie and his parents went to visit his grandmother at Maple Hill back in Worcester. Robbie enjoyed the summers at Maple Hill because he loved his "Gram" very much. Mary Goddard was a cheerful woman who looked to the future and did not cling to "the good old days." She thought today was just fine and tomorrow would be splendid. Madam Goddard was the opposite of the generations of dour New Englanders from whom she had descended. She was determined that Robert would look to the future and not to the past.

Just as Robbie's father had interested his son in new inventions, he took advantage of these vacations to teach Robbie to enjoy nature. They tramped together in the woods around Worcester and fished in the ponds.

But close as he was to his father, Robbie took after his

Robbie sitting between his father and mother at Maple Hill in 1890. His grandmother, Mary Pease Upham Goddard, is standing behind him.

mother. He was often sick, which left him thin and pale. By the time he was ready to go to high school, he was two grades behind other students his own age. Even near the end of the nineteenth century, there was little medical science could do for sick people. Living was survival of the fittest, and Robbie Goddard was not very fit.

Robbie, because he was sick so much, turned to reading books. But good books were not cheap, and public libraries were thinly stocked. Some newspapers printed daily installments of new and interesting books to increase the number of papers they sold everyday. In January 1898, the Boston *Post* printed chapter by chapter *Fighters from Mars, or The War of the Worlds, in and near Boston,* a new book by the English writer H. G. Wells. The action of Wells's book was set in the late 1890s, which made the story all the more exciting. The author included the most up-to-date, scientific beliefs about Mars—its ice caps and seasonal changes and its "canals," which could be seen through telescopes from Earth. Wells wove all this into a realistic here-and-now tale. It carried the frightened but thrilled reader right along with the hero in hairbreadth escapes from the monster Martian invaders of Earth.

The story fascinated Robbie. He was especially interested in Wells's new scientific ideas and descriptions. Wells depicted the Martians encased in large, bullet-shaped cylinders being shot into space by oversized artillery guns. He wrote that if Martians could reach Venus it would not be impossible for humans to travel to other planets, too. Ideas like that fired Robbie's imagination. He never forgot that book.

After reading *War of the Worlds,* Robbie decided he wanted a balloon—not an ordinary rubber balloon, which was readily available, but a permanent balloon that would never leak air or pop. He thought that the best kind should be made of a thin, light metal and filled with hydrogen gas. He bought a quarter pound of aluminum and tried to melt it over the Goddards' kitchen stove. He planned to roll the metal into a thin sheet. But despite his daily effort, the aluminum would not melt. He finally bought a three-foot sheet of aluminum, formed it into a pillow shape, and sealed the edges with litharge—a material made of lead— and glycerin before trying to fill it with hydrogen. He tried and tried to get enough of the gas into the balloon. But the aluminum proved to be too heavy, and the balloon remained earthbound. Nahum Goddard encouraged his son's curiosity. He gave him a telescope, a microscope, money for supplies, and subscriptions to science magazines from which Robbie got ideas for experiments.

When Robert entered Boston English High School in the fall of 1898, his botany teacher, Mr. J. Y. Bergen, became interested in his student's experiments. Robert had read about how to make artificial diamonds and had actually produced some crystals that he showed to his teacher. Bergen encouraged further investigations. While Robert was experimenting in his room, he created a terrific explosion through a miscalculation or inexperience. Tubes were driven into the ceiling; pieces of glass flew all over the house. Robert was not hurt, but on orders from his father he did not attempt such an experiment again.

That same year his mother developed tuberculosis, or TB, a contagious bacterial infection of the lungs. TB was also called consumption, or the white plague, because it was so widespread and a major cause of death in the United States. In 1898, there was no cure, and the only hope for arresting the progress of the disease was rest and fresh air. The doctors advised Fannie Goddard to return to Worcester where the air was cleaner.

Fannie Goddard's doctors also examined her sickly son but could not decide if he had stomach problems or kidney disease. They advised an operation. Robert's parents refused because they knew how dangerous surgery was. Instead, Robert left school again to recover.

During the next year, Nahum Goddard sold his business and the house in Roxbury. The whole family moved back to Maple Hill in Worcester. Nahum returned to the L. Hardy Company as a shop superintendent. His father-in-law was no longer an owner.

Robert didn't mind moving back to Worcester. Maple Hill was like a second home to him. The Goddards lived on the top floor of the house. The first floor was rented to friends Ella and George Boswell. "Uncle" George Boswell was wonderfully handy about fixing things, and his workshop with its tools and pieces of wire, wood, and metal was sheer heaven to Robert.

Uncle George had been helping Robert over the previous four or five summers with Robert's plans for a frog hatchery, a moneymaking project to be built on the brook and pond behind Maple Hill. Frog legs were a popular item on the menus of Boston restaurants. Robert had drawn up detailed plans for electric generators to be harnessed to a wheel turned by the running waters of the brook. He planned to have the tadpoles live in a one-by-three-foot house painted gray with red trim and real glass windows. However, Robert could never seem to stay well long enough to get his plans off the drawing board and into the pond.

When he could, Robert tried to help Uncle George.

One October afternoon, October 19, 1899, to be exact, Robert gathered up a saw, a hatchet, and a ladder he had made and set off to prune a cherry tree behind the barn. It was a beautiful New England fall day. He soon laid aside his tools to enjoy the beauty nature had spread before him from his vantage point up in the tree. As he looked up at the clear blue sky, he again thought about H. G. Wells's book. Wouldn't it be wonderful to make a machine that could go to Mars? He realized it would have to be very large, but he imagined what a small model might be like. "It seemed to me then that a weight whirling around a horizontal shaft, moving more rapidly above than below, could furnish lift by virtue of the greater centrifugal force at the top of the path. In any event, I was a different boy when I descended the tree from when I ascended, for existence at last seemed very purposive."

A 1900 photograph of the cherry tree where Robert H. Goddard the previous year had had his idea about developing a machine that could travel beyond the Earth's atmosphere.

2

"Aiming at the Stars"

Robert fell ill again and had to be in bed several months to recuperate. He tried making wooden models with lead weights whirling around in horizontal arcs like the vehicle he had imagined while he had been up in the cherry tree the previous autumn. In an effort to educate himself, he started reading books and magazines about physics and chemistry.

His father gave him a book called *Popular Education*. In this book, he read about Newton's laws of motion. Sir Isaac Newton, who had lived in the second half of the seventeenth century, was an English scientist, astronomer, and mathematician who had devised calculus. He is most famous for his theory of gravity and his three laws of motion. The first law concerns overcoming inertia—a body in motion in a straight line will remain in motion; a body at rest will remain at rest. The second law states that the change any force makes in the motion of any object depends on the size of the force and the size and density of the object. It was Newton's third law that really fascinated Robert Goddard. For every action, there is an equal and opposite reaction. He knew somehow he had to apply that law to his dreams of flight. Having taken only a year of high school algebra so far, he realized there was little he could do until he learned more. He vowed that if he ever got back into school he would master physics and even math, which he hated. For he had decided what he wanted to do with the rest of his life: high-altitude research. To learn to do that, self-education was not enough.

In the fall of 1900, Robert tried to return to school by enrolling part-time in Becker's Business College in Worcester. It wasn't long before even this reduced schedule was too much for him. He suffered a relapse and had to drop out of school again. At home for another year, he read, sent away for anything written about flight, and dreamed.

While he rested outside on good weather days, he studied the flight of birds and how the balancing mechanism in their inner ears allowed them to soar and dive. He wondered if it would be possible to duplicate this balance mechanically through a series of gyroscopes. A gyroscope consists of a wheel called a rotor that spins on its axle like a child's top. Unlike a top, however, a gyroscope is mounted in a frame that allows it to stay on one plane once it starts to spin, even if the surface beneath it tilts or moves. The frame is made of two rings, one vertical and the other horizontal, called gimbals. The rotor axle is suspended in the gimbal frame by pins so that it can spin freely.

Robert thought the gyroscopes' unshakability once

they started turning could be used as a propulsion force to lift a space vehicle. But he discarded this idea when he found the force of a gyroscope might steady a ship but was not enough to propel even a small vehicle upward. Yet he wrote up his experiments with gyroscopes and filed them away with his ever-growing collection of papers, perhaps to be used another time.

Finally in 1901, Robert was declared fit enough to try school again. But by now he was four years older than other sophomores in high school. He should have been entering his sophomore year in college. How could he, a nineteen-year-old grown-up, attend school with fifteen-year-old children, he protested; he wouldn't fit in. After much arguing, he agreed to *try* newly built South High.

South High School was not only new, but it also practiced some new ideas in education. Students could specialize in subjects they liked and get extra help from teachers. Robert became good friends with his physics teacher, Calvin Andrews. Andrews was interested in astronomy, the study of the universe beyond the earth's atmosphere. Robert, at last, had someone he could talk to about H. G. Wells's wonderful books and his own dreams— someone who understood and would not laugh at him. Even on summer evenings when school was out, Robert was invited to sit on Calvin Andrew's front porch. They talked about outer space as they watched the moon, planets, and stars move across the night sky.

During the years he spent in high school, Robert wrote about his ideas in articles he sent to magazines for possible publication. They were rejected. He wrote to the Smithsonian Institution in Washington, D.C., for answers to his questions on space. But Robert had questions even the Smithsonian could not answer.

Robert did not spend all his time reading and dreaming "what-if" space dreams. Despite his misgivings, he was admired by his younger classmates at South High School. Twice they elected him class president. If that didn't keep him busy enough, he also edited the school paper, participated in the debating society, played the piano at class parties and shows, and took dancing lessons. He wrote in his diary, "Went to leap-year dance in evening. Very great? All very very great!!"

Robert was valedictorian of his class in 1904, so he had to give a speech at graduation. He titled it "On Taking

Robert H. Goddard's 1904 high school graduation photograph.

Things for Granted." Of course he managed to get in a few lines about space, and he closed the speech with the prediction that "it has often proved true that the dream of yesterday is the hope of today and the reality of tomorrow."

Not long after graduating from high school, twenty-two-year-old Robert Goddard tried to face the hard fact that his dreams and hopes of flight beyond the atmosphere had no chance for reality. He gathered up his notes and models and burned them in the wood stove. Yet he soon wrote, "But the dream would not 'down,' and inside of two months I caught myself making notes of further suggestions, for even though I reasoned with myself that the thing [space travel] was impossible, there was something inside which simply would not stop working."

Robert Goddard seemed to have no choice but to continue his study of the possibility of space flight. In a scientific manner, he would go about this mission thrust on him by fate. He bought a set of green cloth-covered notebooks and started recording all his ideas (which he called suggestions) and his experiments, even the failures.

But to continue, he had to learn still more. He knew that if his ideas on space were ever to become fact he would have to study physics and other sciences at a great university. But his parents were weighed down by the medical bills from his mother's worsening health and could not afford to send him. Practicality won out. Although Robert was not truly interested in an engineering career, he enrolled at Worcester Polytechnic Institute. It was a college that taught young men engineering skills to supply the needs of the city's many industries. His grandmother Mary Goddard, who had only a tiny Civil War widow's pension to live on, borrowed money to pay his tuition. She thought her grandson should follow his dream.

Soon after starting classes at "Tech," his physics professor, Dr. A. Wilmer Duff, recognized Robert Goddard's abilities and hired him as his laboratory assistant. He also recommended Robert Goddard as a tutor so he was able to earn some badly needed extra money.

Goddard constantly questioned Duff and his other professors in order to learn more facts to solve the problems of space travel. When the professors asked why he wanted to know things that had little or nothing to do with the subject being studied, Goddard backed away. He would not reveal to anyone except his family and a few others his dreams of space. Such ideas were not accepted by serious scientists. Space was the territory of fiction writers like H. G. Wells and Jules Verne, whose books Goddard read again and again.

Yet he continued to fill his green notebooks with ideas, questions, and information. His first problem was boosting a vehicle into space, but Goddard also wondered how it would get back to Earth without burning up in the atmosphere. How would humans survive the tremendous speeds? How would they breathe in the vacuum beyond Earth's oxygen-rich atmosphere? What about meteors? Would it be possible for a spaceship to avoid collision by traveling within "a meteor swarm"? In frustration he wrote in his diary in 1906 that he had "decided today that space navigation is a physical impossibility." But the dream would not "down" for long.

Goddard's fellow students thought he was brilliant. The class of 1908 elected him class vice-president freshman year and class president sophomore year. He was also class secretary and was always being put on various school committees. Since he was several years older than most of his classmates, Goddard possessed a maturity they did not have yet. Despite the age difference, he was asked to join a social fraternity.

He really flabbergasted the other sophomore engineering students when their English professor gave them the assignment of writing a paper on the topic "Travelling in 1950." Goddard's theme was a fictional short story called "The High-Speed Bet." It was about a man who, because of a wager, builds a high-speed train that travels in a 200-mile-long vacuum tube. Goddard explained within the framework of the story just how the train with no rails, no wheels, and no engine would make the trip from Boston to New York City in ten minutes by the push-pull force of electromagnets in the walls of the tunnel and on the train. He even had the electricity in the magnets generated by motors powered by waves off the coast of Long Island.

For another theme for his English class, Goddard dusted off his old ideas about gyroscopes and wrote "The Use of the Gyroscope in the Balancing and Steering of Airplanes." When Professor Duff read it, he encouraged Goddard to revise it and send it to *Scientific American* magazine, for Duff had never heard of a gyrostabilizer used in this way before. The magazine published the article in its supplement on June 29, 1907, and paid Goddard ten dollars.

Thinking his luck had changed, Goddard sent off to *Scientific American* another article, "On the Possibility of Navigating Interplanetary Space." This time the magazine sent a personal rejection with some suggestions for improving it. Undiscouraged, Goddard sent the article to *Popular Astronomy*. That magazine also rejected it. In its reply the magazine editor said that while Goddard had "written well" the possibility of what he proposed was so "remote," it was not helpful to science. Science was not ready for ideas like getting a vehicle into space by using solar energy and atomic force, liquid propellants, or even electricity. Goddard's suggestion of sending a camera around the planets to photograph them close up and bring the pictures back was considered preposterous—in 1907.

The study of space was not recognized as an academic subject, so there were no courses in it at Tech. Goddard's space work had to remain a hobby. Instead, he studied electrical engineering. In 1908, he wrote a graduation thesis entitled "On Some Peculiarities of Electrical Conductivity Exhibited by Powders and a Few Solid Substances." It was based on the working principle of Marconi's wireless. Goddard's practical future seemed to lie in engineering the further development of radio.

He graduated first in his class, which earned him a seventy-five-dollar prize. He needed all the money he could get because he wanted to earn a doctor of philosophy degree in physics—and that meant more years of study. Goddard had to postpone going to Clark University in Worcester for a year. To support himself and save money, he took a teaching job at Worcester Polytechnic Institute.

To follow his "dream," Robert Goddard had to pay a price. Part of that price was losing the woman he loved. For Robert fell in love with Miriam Olmstead as the two honor students representing the class of 1904 at South High School rehearsed their graduation speech. That summer they spent time walking in the park and talking of their ambitions for the future. In the fall, Robert Goddard enrolled at Worcester Polytechnic while Miriam went off to Smith College. They wrote almost daily letters to each other, and by Thanksgiving of 1905, Goddard gave Miriam Olmstead a small diamond ring. But by the time they graduated from college, they had grown apart. Goddard insisted he would have to earn his doctorate, get a teaching position, and save some money before he could marry. Miriam Olmstead went off to study in Europe.

At Clark University during the fall of 1909, Goddard started his study of advanced physics, a science concerned with nonliving matter and energy as well as motion and force. Newton's three laws of motion are laws of physics. Yet Goddard, even at Clark, had to study the physics of electricity, not space. His master's degree thesis was entitled "Theory of Diffraction." It dealt with the bending of light and sound waves around obstacles in their path. The thesis was a continuation of the work he had done at Tech.

After another year of intensive work, Goddard earned his doctoral degree—cum laude (with honors)—on June 15, 1911. His answers during the oral examination conducted by a committee of Clark University professors to test his knowledge were called brilliant. His thesis again was in the field of electricity: "On the Conduction at Contacts of Dissimilar Solids."

Dr. Robert H. Goddard, with his student days behind him at last, went in search of work. He had been offered a $1,000-a-year job to teach at the University of Missouri and $1,600 a year to teach at the renowned Columbia University in New York City. But he turned these down because he would have had to spend most of his time teaching and would not have had enough time to do research. Research on space travel was so important to Dr.

Goddard that he accepted a position at Clark University as an honorary fellow in physics. This meant he could use the laboratory facilities for research, but he received no salary.

The year 1912 was important to Goddard. He worked out the theory and mathematical formulas for using smokeless powders and hydrogen and oxygen as rocket propellants. His calculations told him he would need 43.5 pounds of hydrogen and oxygen to send 1 pound beyond the reach of gravity. But that was in theory. In practice, liquid hydrogen was unobtainable and liquid oxygen scarce because to become liquid, these gases had to be cooled to hundreds of degrees below zero.

Dr. Goddard also did a number of experiments with electricity. He sent electrical charges—subatomic-sized particles called electrons and ions—through a vacuum in a cathode tube (somewhat similar to the picture tube used in television sets today). He found the electrons and ions exerted a backward force, or reaction. It was an example of Newton's third law—for every action there is an opposite and equal reaction. What excited Goddard was that this electrical force worked in a vacuum. He knew that once a space vehicle leaves Earth's atmosphere it must travel in the vacuum of outer space. How wonderful it would be, he thought, if this force could be generated in a lightweight engine in order to propel a space vehicle. He wrote about his experiments to the secretary of the American Physical Society, an important scientific group that was to have a meeting in two weeks at Harvard University. The secretary wrote back at once inviting Dr. Goddard to present the results of his work at the society's meeting.

But when Dr. Goddard tried to repeat his experiment in his laboratory, he found he had made a dreadful mistake. Instead of the electrical charge of electrons and ions reacting with force against the vacuum, they had been reacting against a wire he had not noticed.

With the help of Dr. H. F. Stimson, a fellow physicist, Goddard set up another experiment. This time they tried for a reaction or force from a stream of electrons and ions acting against a dielectric, or non-electricity-conducting, material like hard rubber, which also could be used in a vacuum. The experiment worked. Goddard and Stimson tried it again and again with the same result. With less than twenty-four hours before he was to appear at Harvard, Dr. Goddard had to write up the complicated mathematical formulas and procedures into a speech.

The other physicists listened to the speech with great interest. Dr. W. F. Magie, dean of the Palmer Physical Laboratory at Princeton University, was so impressed by Goddard's work that he offered the twenty-nine-year-old scientist a position on the Princeton faculty as a research instructor at a salary of $1,000 a year. Goddard was delighted with the idea of being able to do experiments at these well-equipped laboratories and to work with other scientists looking into the power of electricity. He took up his work at Princeton in the fall of 1912. Grandmother Goddard, never too old to want to try something new, went with him to keep house and make sure he got good food and rest.

In the daytime, Dr. Goddard continued to work on the electrical experiment he had talked about at Harvard. His work laid the foundation for vacuum radio tubes invented by later researchers. He conducted his experiments in a sealed gas chamber that he had rigged up. The chamber was filled with the fumes of the sulfuric acid he used. The fumes were irritating to breathe, and he suffered from coughing while conducting the experiments.

On his own time during the evenings, Dr. Goddard worked on ways to propel a vehicle into space, at least in theory. He did further work on the ideas he had experimented with at Tech. Gases generated by burning smokeless powders might give off enough energy to propel a vehicle into space. Mathematically, he calculated these methods could give him a burning efficiency (the amount of energy given off per pound of fuel burned) of 50 to 70 percent, which he needed so the space vehicle would not be weighted down with too much fuel. Night after night he pondered his ideas and worked them out mathematically. He proved to himself it would be possible for a vehicle to overcome the pull of gravity and the pressure of the atmosphere. With this 50 percent or better efficiency, he calculated it would take about five hundred pounds of thrust, or push against gravity from the fuel burning in the engine, to boost one pound into space.

Dr. Goddard loved working days and especially nights in his laboratory at Princeton University. But such intense effort was hard on him. He caught colds that were, as he said, "peculiar." He had yet another cold when he left Princeton on March 19, 1913, to spend his spring vacation with his parents in Worcester.

Dr. Goddard was no sooner home than his cold became much worse. The doctor's diagnosis was not a bad cold, but the dreaded tuberculosis—a case so far advanced there was no hope. He gave Robert Goddard a week or two at the most to live.

3

Skyrockets

People can carry the tuberculosis bacteria in their bodies for years, yet remain well. The bacteria will encapsulate and remain dormant until the person is weakened by other illnesses. Then the TB bacteria may become active causing cells in the lungs to die, leaving holes in the lung tissue. TB can also affect other parts of the body, like the joints, bones, and skin. TB was still a widespread disease in the first half of the twentieth century.

When Robert Goddard's TB became active, he refused to die. For two weeks he was racked with high fevers and constant coughing that exhausted him. The doctors had some standard treatments for TB. One was splashing ice water on the patient's chest; another was having the patient sleep on an open porch even during New England winters. With his scientist's mind, Goddard thought these treatments were silly, even harmful. He refused to follow his doctor's orders and treated himself by deep breathing exercises and sleeping in his room with the heat on. He did agree to leave the windows open.

Goddard's self-treatment worked. In two weeks, instead of being dead, he was better. But he was so weak that he had to follow his doctor's orders to remain as quiet as possible. Unable even to pick up a pen and write, he dictated a letter to his father requesting his grandmother still in Princeton "to pack up all my belongings and to pack away every scrap of paper."

Robert Goddard hid his papers from his nurse under his mattress and his pillow. When his temperature came down to the point where his mind could function clearly again, he allowed himself one hour's work a day. Having that one hour was the incentive that helped him strive toward getting better. During the rest of the day, he would think, calculate, and plan. As with the illnesses in his childhood, the thinking time was not wasted. He had worked out his theory of how to propel an object into space flight mathematically while he was at Princeton. Now he determined he was ready to put this theory into practice and make a real space vehicle—a rocket. But first he had to get back on his feet.

He devised his own methods to regain his health. It was slow. He was not able to go downstairs in his house for two months. His first drive in his father's automobile lasted only twelve minutes. Then he began taking walks, trying to go a few feet farther every day.

A year later, Dr. Goddard still had not recovered his full strength. His illness had left him bald at the age of thirty-two. He weighed only 136 pounds, though he was of average height. His parents insisted he see a parade of doctors, all of whom were amazed he was alive. They prescribed all sorts of health plans that seemed to guarantee he would be an invalid for the rest of his life.

He knew he did not have the strength to return to doing research at Princeton University full-time, although Dean Magie wanted him back. Instead, in 1914 Dr. Goddard was able to arrange to teach a course in electricity and magnetism three hours a week as an instructor at Clark University for $500 a year. This schedule earned him a little money and left him time for his own experiments.

While he was making his recovery, Dr. Goddard began to collect rockets. Rockets have shot skyward since the Chinese invented them in the thirteenth century. The Chinese tightly packed saltpeter (sodium nitrate gathered from the droppings of bats found in limestone caves) and charcoal into a capped cylinder made of leather or into hollow bamboo tubes. These were attached to arrows or spears or just sticks for guidance and balance. When the charcoal and saltpeter were lighted, the fuel burned just at the surface. It did not explode all at once. The tube was pushed skyward by the burning gases that rushed out of a narrow opening at one end. The Chinese used these "arrows of flying fire" against the invading Mongols. The idea spread quickly from China along the trade routes to India, Arabia, and Europe. Around the same time, gunpowder was invented. It was a combination of sulfur, charcoal, and potash that burned rapidly. When gunpowder was put into a metal tube and ignited, it could push out an iron ball with great speed and force; this idea was used to develop guns. Fiery rockets were used in wars in many parts of the world, more for the scare they could give to the enemy than for the damage they could do. However, they were useful in setting fire to fortifications.

In the early nineteenth century, Sir William Congreve

of England made rockets that carried explosive warheads weighing up to forty or fifty pounds. They could fly more than a mile. These were the kinds of rockets used by the British against the American-held Fort Henry off Baltimore, Maryland, in the War of 1812. The American lawyer, Francis Scott Key, who was an eyewitness to that battle, wrote about "the rockets' red glare" in his poem that became "The Star-Spangled Banner." Armies all over the world used Congreve rockets during the first half of the nineteenth century. By about 1860, they were considered obsolete. A line-carrying rocket was invented in the early 1800s to rescue people at sea. It could send a lifeline out to drowning people and ships wrecked near coastlines. It saved thousands of lives.

In Russia, the scientist Konstantin Tsiolkovsky became interested in space travel. He was a self-taught mathematician and physicist who in 1898 figured out the possibility of rocket motion by mathematical formulas. These laws of mathematics were the basis for the design of any rocket. In 1903 Tsiolkovsky published *Investigations of Space by Means of Rockets*, a book about interplanetary flight using rocket power. His work was little known outside Russia. Even though that country was involved in the Russo-Japanese War of 1904–5, World War I, the overthrow of the czar, and the establishment of communism, the various Russian governments took a great interest in Tsiolkovsky's work. He was given high honors and a state funeral in 1935.

Rockets all work on the same principle. Burning fuels inside the rocket give off a gas. The gas escaping from the back of a rocket creates an unequal pressure on one side. The remaining stronger pressure inside causes the rocket to move forward. A common way to demonstrate this principle is by inflating an ordinary balloon. When one holds the stem of the balloon shut, the pressure is equal on all sides. But if the person lets go, the balloon will be propelled forward as the air escapes from the opening. It is not the rush of air out of the balloon pushing against the outside air that makes the balloon move; rather, it is the sudden unequal pressure inside that propels it. The narrower the opening for the air to come out, the more force it has.

Goddard explained it this way: "Rockets are propelled not at all by 'kicking against the air,' but by the recoil from the high-speed ejected gases. It is exactly like the recoil of a shotgun."

Goddard kept on sending away for rockets. He was especially interested in signal rockets used by the U.S. Navy. All the rockets he had collected were really the Fourth of July variety. A fuse was lighted, which ignited a gunpowder mixture called black powder, and the gases created by the burn sent the rocket up with a whoosh. While these fireworks were pretty to look at, only about 2 percent of the energy created by their burning fuel went into sending them at 1,000 feet per second into the air. Goddard knew from his mathematical calculations that he had to get at least a 50-percent efficiency from fuels for a rocket to be thrust beyond Earth's gravity and atmospheric pressures. Goddard made his own rockets of steel one-half to one inch in diameter and up to a foot long. He sent away for newer types of explosives, smokeless powders, and gunpowder. It wasn't just the type of fuel that would create maximum lift. The shape of the narrow opening the gases were forced through also made a difference. Goddard designed nozzles through which the gases could be expelled at the back of the rockets. These nozzles were smooth, highly polished, tapered tubes, and they took up half the

Dr. Robert H. Goddard with a steel combustion chamber and a rocket nozzle. This photograph was taken in 1915.

length of his rockets. Just as with the balloon experiment, the smaller the opening for gases to escape, the greater the forward thrust. He got a fuel efficiency of 64 percent in actual experiments.

Goddard fired off a few of his small rockets outside the physics building on the Clark University campus. But the noise and the fireworks caused so much alarm that he had to move his experiments to the more remote Coes Pond on the edge of Worcester. On June 16, 1915, one of his modified rockets went up 486 feet at a speed he calculated to be 8,000 feet per second. It was a big improvement over a Fourth of July rocket.

Robert Goddard decided he had better patent his ideas. Working with lawyer Charles T. Hawley of Worcester, who specialized in helping people obtain patents, Goddard sent detailed drawings of his ideas to the U.S. Patent Office in Washington, D.C. In 1914 the Patent Office determined that no one else had been given a patent on anything like what Dr. Goddard had submitted. It sent him an official patent, a document with a number assigned to his invention. This was supposed to prevent anyone else from making, using, or selling Goddard's invention without his permission. People would have to pay him a royalty (money) for the use of the invention. However, patents are only granted for seventeen years. Two patents—No. 1,102,653 and No. 1,103,503—were granted to Goddard for "rocket apparatus." The patents covered three things: several methods of feeding different kinds of liquids or solid propellants into a combustion chamber, the chamber itself, and a nozzle to the outside to expel the gases. He also patented his idea for the use of multistage rockets, each stage or section being dropped off as the propellant, or fuel, it contained was used up. These patents covered

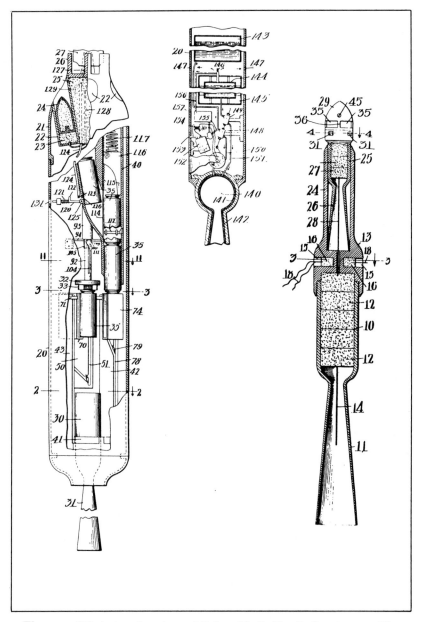

These are U.S. patent drawings of Robert H. Goddard's first patents. They show a multiple-charge solid-propellant rocket, a liquid-propellant rocket, and a step rocket and nozzle.

what became known as the Goddard rocket. The space age had been born, and Dr. Robert Goddard was its father—at least in the United States.

Goddard's next experiments included firing off small rockets in a partial vacuum he rigged up. He wrote that "the less air, the faster the gases escape, and the greater is the propelling force.... The force of recoil was found to be about 22 percent greater in a vacuum than in the air." Goddard was pleased with these results, for they showed that his theories were proving true in practice.

He wrote up his mathematical calculations and experiments in a scientific paper entitled "The Problem of Raising a Body to a Great Altitude Above the Surface of the Earth." At the beginning of the paper, Goddard stated the purpose: "The problem is concerned with the practicability of doing two things, namely: raising of apparatus, such as recording instruments, to a great altitude, and letting it fall back to the ground by suitable parachutes; and second, the sending of apparatus to such great distances from the earth that the apparatus comes under the influence of the gravitational attraction of some other heavenly body"—in other words, sending the "apparatus" to the moon or other planets.

As described in his paper, Goddard's method of sending an "apparatus" into space was based on the ideas covered by his patents. The energy sources he proposed would be smokeless powders like gun cotton (an explosive made of cotton soaked in chemicals that gives off a large force of energy but does not explode uncontrollably). The other source of energy was liquid hydrogen and oxygen, because small amounts burn quickly and give off great heat energy, *"provided the gas were ejected from the rocket at a high velocity*, and also provided that *most of the rocket consisted of propellant material."*

Goddard also proposed putting a charge of flash powder on a rocket to the moon that would be set off when it impacted. The explosion would be seen by a powerful telescope from Earth to prove that the rocket had reached its destination. He said he had even done calculations and some small experiments with flash powder, but it was not "of obvious scientific importance."

Goddard read his paper before a large audience of students, professors, and other interested people at Clark University. Some reporters from the local newspapers were there. They wrote a short article about his "machine" designed to study the upper atmosphere and beyond.

Morning, noon, and night, day after day, Dr. Goddard worked on his experiments with different explosive powders and nozzles to expel the gases with the greatest force. He read H. G. Wells's book *First Men in the Moon* (1901). Is it any wonder that his work and the book may have influenced him to have a dream in which he went to the moon? Perhaps only a scientist could dream such a realistic dream. In it Goddard imagined it was cold, there was not enough oxygen to breathe (factually there's none on the moon), and he was wearing a helmet.

Pleased with Goddard's work, the trustees of Clark University made him an assistant professor in 1915 and raised his pay to $1,125 per year. He needed the money because he paid for all the materials he used for his experiments out of his own pocket. He did all the work himself with some help from his fellow professors in the physics department. Sometimes workers at his father's company made parts for him without charge. But Goddard

31

could not go on begging for help, and his own savings were exhausted.

On September 27, 1916, Goddard typed a letter to the secretary of the Smithsonian Institution in Washington, D.C. In the letter he appealed for funds to carry on his work. Briefly he outlined what he had done: "For a number of years I have been at work upon a method of raising recording apparatus to altitudes exceeding the limit for sounding balloons." (Sounding balloons could go up 20 to 25 miles. It was thought at that time that Earth's atmosphere extended upward about 200 miles instead of the actual 1,000 miles discovered years later.) He closed his letter with this plea, "I realize that in sending this communication, I have taken a certain liberty; but I feel that it is to the Smithsonian Institution alone that I must look, now that I cannot continue the work unassisted."

The Smithsonian Institution had been established by an 1846 act of Congress through an 1829 gift of half million dollars to the U.S. government from James Smithson, an Englishman. He had been a leading scientist of his time in Europe, but he had never been to the United States. He specified in his will, "I then bequeath the whole of my property...to the United States of America, to found at Washington, under the name of the Smithsonian Institution, an establishment for the increase and diffusion of knowledge among men." Since that time, the Smithsonian has aided research and exploration, displayed collections and historic items, as well as published scientific information as it was directed to do by Smithson.

The directors of the Smithsonian were interested in Goddard's ideas. He sent them his manuscript entitled, "A Method of Sending Recording Apparatus to, and Beyond, the Highest Levels of the Atmosphere." In the paper he described his methods, calculations, and discoveries in detail. The Smithsonian had supported flight research since aviation pioneer Samuel Langley had been its secretary beginning in 1887. The secretary and head of the Smithsonian at the time of Goddard's request, Dr. Charles D. Walcott, was instrumental in getting Congress to fund aeronautical research and establish the National Advisory Committee for Aeronautics (NACA) in 1915. After studying and checking his research, the Smithsonian, on January 5, 1917, granted Goddard $5,000 to carry on his research for a year.

Goddard's grandmother, who had encouraged him from the time he was a child right up to the end of her life, did not live to see this recognition of his work. She died on October 17, 1916.

4

The Cloak-and-Dagger Caper

While Dr. Robert Goddard was making his slow recovery from tuberculosis, Europe was rapidly heading for war. On June 28, 1914, Archduke Francis Ferdinand of Austria-Hungary, the heir apparent (future emperor and king), was assassinated in Sarajevo, Serbia (part of present-day Yugoslavia). On July 28, Austria-Hungary declared war on Serbia. Within days, Germany declared war on Russia, France, and Belgium. Great Britain declared war on Germany, and World War I was on.

Goddard wrote to U.S. Secretary of the Navy Josephus Daniels about using his rocket as an antiaircraft weapon, an antitank weapon, or even a torpedo. Within a week he received a letter from Assistant Secretary of the Navy Franklin D. Roosevelt. He said the navy was interested in Goddard's ideas but wanted a demonstration of the devices at the Naval Torpedo Station at Newport, Rhode

Island. Goddard knew he was still too weak from his bout with TB to build a model. He wrote back saying, "I should like to take advantage of the offer sometime later if it is a possible thing."

President Woodrow Wilson, who had been president of Princeton University when Goddard was there, was determined to keep the country out of the war. He said the United States "must be neutral in fact as well as in name....We must be impartial in thought as well as action." But in 1915, German submarines sank the British liner *Lusitania*, and 128 Americans were among the 1,198 passengers who died. Later, submarines sank unarmed American merchant ships. In early 1917 a German plot was uncovered. Germany planned to urge Mexico to be an ally in a war against the United States. Mexico would be promised financial support and would regain territory lost to the United States in the Mexican War of the 1840s. With these constant provocations, on April 6, 1917, the U.S. Congress declared war on Germany.

With his country at war, Dr. Goddard's regular report on the progress of his work to the Smithsonian Institution mentioned the use of his rocket research in making a missile with a long-range capability. But he warned it should be a U.S. government secret.

The people at the Smithsonian agreed with him. But when they approached the U.S. War Department, the admirals and the generals again wanted a demonstration. Goddard could only offer theory and a few super Fourth of July rockets he had made.

In August, Goddard himself wrote to the chief of Army Ordnance with a detailed proposal of the warfare applications of his rocket. A captain from West Point was interested; he saw the benefits of using it on airplanes as a gun capable of precision firing against the enemy and for signals from ships. But after several months, Goddard realized that without a model it was hopeless to interest the War Department itself.

During January 1918, Goddard went to Washington armed with a letter of introduction from Dr. Arthur G. Webster, head of the Clark University physics department. At the same time the Smithsonian wrote to a general in the U.S. Army Signal Corps telling him of Goddard's rocket. Finally in February 1918, ten months after the United States had entered the war, the U.S. Army Signal Corps in cooperation with Army Ordnance agreed to finance Goddard's work to make military rockets.

His old school, Worcester Polytechnic Institute, loaned Dr. Goddard the use of a small building in a far corner of its campus for his war work. With the government behind him, he could afford to hire people to help him: an experienced toolmaker, a chemistry expert (Dr. Henry C. Parker), two machinery designers, three other assistants, and even a high school errand boy. Goddard also found it necessary to hire an armed night watchman, for he seriously believed enemy governments were interested in his work.

Strange people constantly came to the door or peered in at the windows. Goddard had to fire his chief assistant when he thought the man had breached the secrecy with which Goddard surrounded the project. An unknown army colonel arrived in Worcester without any warning on an "inspection trip." Goddard wouldn't let him in his laboratory. Phone calls and telegrams flew between Worcester and Washington as Goddard reported all these goings-on to the Smithsonian and the U.S. Army Signal Corps. They soon decided Dr. Goddard should continue his work at the Mount Wilson Observatory near Pasadena in southern California. Secrecy could be better maintained there, especially when he was ready to test in the open the rocket weapons he was developing.

In cloak-and-dagger fashion, Goddard packed the rocket propellants and critical small parts into his suitcases and sneaked out of Worcester in the middle of the night. He and three of his assistants drove a truck with a piece of canvas over the license plate to Springfield, Massachusetts, where they boarded a train to Chicago. They thought the Worcester train station might be watched. Goddard told the railroad porters his suitcases were filled with TNT so no one would touch them. By June 11, Goddard and his rocket were safely in California. Meanwhile, back in Worcester, Nahum Goddard removed the machinery, tools, and equipment needed to make the rocket to L. Hardy Company, where he had them crated and shipped to Pasadena. As far as anyone else knew, Dr. Goddard had disappeared off the face of the earth.

Dr. Henry C. Parker and Clarence N. Hickman, a graduate student from Clark, went with Dr. Goddard to Pasadena. With an additional $20,000 from the U.S. Army Signal Corps, the three men worked on two main projects: short-range, single-charge rockets and multiple-charge rockets. The work went well, although Clarence Hickman lost part of four of his fingers in accidents while working on the rockets. By July 9, Goddard had tested the single-charge rocket propelled by nitroglycerin powder in the canyons near Mount Wilson. It went straight up out of the canyon. This was one of many versions he developed and tested. Each one was a little different from the others so that he could find the formula that worked best.

The longer Goddard worked with the rocket, the more

military uses he could see for it. An immediate one was as a trench mortar with four times the range of the trench mortars then being used against Germany on the battle-fields of France. A trench mortar was a short, wide-mouthed, heavy cannon that could fire shells in a high arc. Goddard's model was almost six feet long. But although it weighed only six pounds, it could fire an eight-pound shell. A soldier could carry it and even fire it from his shoulder. Goddard also saw his rocket adaptable as an airplane gun and on submarines because of its light recoil.

With the success of these tests, Goddard knew he was on the right track. He had the money, but what he needed were more scientists and engineers to help him. He had to beg and borrow physicists from Clark University and army research sites for a few weeks at a time. Goddard knew it was essential to the war effort to get these revolutionary weapons into production and onto the battlefield. But he could not get the help he needed. Other things slowed his progress.

Goddard reached the point where he needed some-one from the army to see his tests so that person could tell him how to tailor the rocket devices for better military applications.

Finally, two army captains came to Mount Wilson on September 13 and 14, 1918, to see what kind of "toys" the professor had come up with. They were amazed. Professor Goddard's rockets were going to revolutionize warfare. After reading the captains' reports about the wonder weapons, the army generals wanted to see Goddard's in-ventions in action at the Aberdeen Proving Grounds in Maryland, a testing place for artillery, mortars, and other military hardware. Goddard packed up his devices and headed by train cross-country to Maryland.

This 1918 forerunner of the bazooka is loaded with a three-inch projectile. Dr. Robert H. Goddard developed this weapon at the Mount Wilson Observatory in California.

He reached Aberdeen on October 26, and with his assistants, Hickman and Parker, he began setting up the weapons. On November 6 several officers representing the Signal Corps and Army Ordnance, the director of the Bureau of Standards, and Dr. Charles G. Abbot of the Smithsonian were ready and waiting at Aberdeen. This is Goddard's part of the weapons demonstration held that day.

Wednesday Afternoon, November 6, 1918
A. Recoilless Guns—Remarks by Dr. Goddard.
    1. One-inch type
        a. Music-stand demonstration

      (1) Fire from open tube to show absence of recoil

      (2) Fire with unconstricted nozzle to show negative recoil

      (3) Fire with constricted nozzle to show increase in velocity and small recoil

      (4) Fire with constricted plug to show value of nozzle on gun

      (5) Fire with spiral nozzle to show rotation

   b. Recoilless hand gun

      (1) Fire gun to illustrate manner in which guns may be fired

      (2) Fire projectile with heavy head to show flight

  2. Two-inch type

    a. Fire with large nozzle on gun

    b. Fire with small nozzle on gun

B. Double-expansion Guns

  1. Double-expansion gun

    a. Fire one round with light head

    b. Fire one round with heavy head to show pressures and muzzle energy

  2. Double-expansion trench mortar

    a. Fire one shot at short range

    b. Fire one shot at long range, to show method of varying the range

C. Multiple-charge Projectiles

  1. Piston-loading device

    a. Fire small type

    b. Fire large type

    c. Suggestions for large number of charges

  2. Explosive-loading type

Goddard and his assistants fired off one-, two-, and three-inch-bore recoilless-type rocket launchers. (The term *recoilless* meant there was little or no kickback to the launcher when it fired. Recoil could be a serious problem when firing any type of gun.) Goddard's launchers fired off warheads weighing between five and fifty pounds. They also fired rockets from small launchers. Hickman created excitement by holding one in his hands and under his arm to prove how easily they could be used as personal artillery by individual soldiers. Another single rocket, fired from a long tube supported by frail music stands and traveling at 750 miles an hour, went through a sandbox and two layers of sandbags behind it. It was immediately seen as an effective antitank weapon. Goddard explained in his "suggestions" in the program that the multiple-charge weapons needed more work. These were many weapons to be developed in nine months.

Immediately, the U.S. Air Service of the War Department asked Dr. Goddard to adapt his recoilless gun for use as airplane heavy artillery. The U.S. Navy was interested in using Goddard's guns as signal rockets. Goddard went to work drawing up specifications for a four-inch recoilless gun.

On November 11, 1918, at 11:00 A.M., an armistice was declared; the world war was over. Within ten days, the War Department stopped all development work on tools of war. There were vague rumors and talk that new work might be funded again in six months to a year after a reorganization. Instead of returning to Pasadena, Goddard went home to Worcester to teach, research, and wait.

For the next year, Robert Goddard continued to send blueprints to the Army Ordnance Department, the Bureau of Standards, and the Smithsonian Institution. In March

1919, the War Department wrote that no funds were available for experimental work. As far as the government was concerned, the world war had been "a war to end all wars."

The same month, somebody released Goddard's work on rocket weapons to the press. Headlines appeared in the Worcester *Evening Gazette* on March 29, 1919: "INVENTS ROCKET WITH ALTITUDE RANGE 70 MILES Terrible Engine of War Developed in Worcester by Dr. Robert H. Goddard, Professor of Physics at Clark, in Laboratory of Worcester Tech, under Patronage of U.S. War Department."

Although the headline was a vast exaggeration of what Goddard's rockets could do, the article did include descriptions of his secret work done in Worcester before he had left for California as well as information from his patents. It described the single-charged and multicharged rockets. Goddard tried by denials and even legal means to get the stories stopped, but he couldn't. His precious secrecy was lost. This story was on the news wire services and was printed in the Washington *Star* and in foreign newspapers, where some people found it *very interesting*.

Now that the news was out, Dr. Arthur G. Webster, Goddard's superior at Clark University, urged him to publish the paper he had sent to the Smithsonian three years before. Goddard did not want to publish anything about his rocket work until he had a model that would reach very high altitudes. But Dr. Webster insisted, saying he would publish it himself if Goddard did not.

Dr. Goddard wrote to Dr. Abbot at the Smithsonian to see if he wanted to publish his 1916 work. Goddard would have to add updates on his weapons development and on his experiments with the use of hydrogen and liquid oxygen as propellants.

Much to Goddard's surprise, the Smithsonian agreed

to publish the paper. It might bring in new money to support his research. The paper was published in December 1919 under the title *A Method of Reaching Extreme Altitudes*. One thousand seven hundred and fifty copies bound in plain brown paper were printed. Goddard received ninety copies, and others were mailed to people on the Smithsonian Institution's mailing list, mostly scientists, who were the only ones who could understand it. The paper, which was sixty-nine pages long, went into great detail; it contained advanced mathematical calculations, descriptions of experiments already made, and pictures of equipment Goddard had devised and used.

In conclusion, Dr. Goddard wrote:

> Although the present paper is not the description of a working model, it is believed, nevertheless, that the theory and the experiments, herein described, together settle all points that could seriously be questioned, and that it remains only to perform certain necessary preliminary experiments before an apparatus can be constructed that will carry recording instruments to any desired altitude.

On Monday, January 11, 1920, the Smithsonian Institution released a statement to the press that Professor Robert H. Goddard of Clark University had invented a multicharged high-efficiency rocket. The rocket was an entirely new design for taking scientific instruments into Earth's unknown upper atmosphere. The announcement was long but written in nontechnical language. The next day, the story was on the front page of most major newspapers in the United States and a few days later in Europe.

Dr. Goddard had resisted publishing this paper because he knew he was the stereotype of what people thought of as the inventor. He was brilliant; he worked alone or with a few part-time assistants in secret obscurity; he struggled to build his invention in poverty. The work progressed slowly because he did not have enough help or money. Without a rocket that actually did in practice what he proposed could be done in theory, he knew people would not understand. He would be laughed at. On January 12, 1920, Dr. Robert Hutchings Goddard was famous, like it or not.

5

The Moon-Rocket Man

The years after World War I were a time of radical changes in the United States. The decade of the 1920s became known as the "Roaring Twenties." The stock market was up, and many people had money. They bought Henry Ford's inexpensive Model T automobile by the thousands. Americans flocked to motion pictures and lived by the radio. They rejected the sedate ways of the prewar years. Women gained the right to vote, and skirts went from floor length to above the knees. It seemed as if people embraced anything new no matter how crazy.

When the country's most prestigious newspapers like the Chicago *Tribune* had front-page headlines saying, "SCIENCE TO TRY SHOOTING MOON WITH A ROCKET" and "NEW INVENTION MAY PENETRATE SPACE," people were ready to go. They deluged Goddard and the Smithsonian Institution with letters volunteering to ride the first rocket to the moon. From the newspaper stories, everyone seemed to think Goddard had a rocket ready to fly in his backyard, even though he had stated in his paper he did not have a working model. The newspaper reporters ridiculed him as "the moon-rocket man."

Goddard hated the sensationalism. Feeling that the press and the public totally misunderstood him, he issued a statement saying that there had to be much more testing before there could be any possibilities of reaching high altitudes. He wished he had not gone against his own better judgment and had resisted Dr. Webster's insistence that the Smithsonian paper be published. On January 22, 1920, to stop all the nonsense, the world-renowned scientist Dr. Webster had to put his own reputation behind Goddard and publish a letter defending him and his work.

But fame did not mean fortune. Since everyone seemed so interested in his rocket ideas, Goddard proposed raising funds for the purpose of necessary research by a public subscription of $50,000 to $100,000. The money would not go to Goddard directly but would be administered by the Smithsonian Institution. No money was subscribed. He also gave a speech about his rocket research to the American Association of Engineers in order to raise money. The group was most enthusiastic, but no financial support came from it either.

The publication of his work did bring serious interest from some directions. Dr. Alexander Graham Bell, inventor of the telephone, invited Dr. Goddard to come to his home in Washington, D.C. He and his staff had been working on a hydrofoil boat that they had gotten up to a speed of seventy-one miles an hour. He wanted to discuss with Robert Goddard the possibility of using powder explosions to propel the boat through the water faster.

Goddard and Bell had a friendly, informative meeting. Dr. Bell introduced him to his son-in-law, Dr. Gilbert Grosvenor, president of the National Geographic Society. Dr. Grosvenor was most interested in Goddard's rocket research but could not give him National Geographic financial support toward continuing his work.

With his $5,000 from the Smithsonian almost gone, Goddard applied to the trustees of Clark University itself for another $5,000. They promised him $3,500 over the next two years, saying the work when completed would bring recognition to the university. They acknowledged what he had done by making him a full professor and raising his salary to $2,500 a year, with an additional $350 to pay assistants and $650 for supplies.

The publicity revived an interest in Goddard's work by the army and navy. The Bureau of Ordnance of the U.S. Navy wanted him to develop an experimental rocket depth charge. A depth charge is an explosive device for use under water, especially against submarines. It is designed to explode when it reaches a specific depth. The U.S. Navy planned to pay all development costs. Goddard was offered $100 a month plus $15 a day when he worked, and travel expenses. But as part of the conditions, he had to work at the Indian Head Proving Ground in southern Maryland near the Potomac River. Between 1920 and 1923, on school vacations and long weekends, Goddard traveled between Massachusetts and Maryland. He even spent his Christmas break there, working alone much of the time. In three years, Goddard developed a depth-charge rocket for submarine warfare and a powerful rocket with a warhead that could drive a hole through heavy armor plate.

Dr. Goddard didn't seem to mind the loneliness. He could get away from the press and curiosity seekers.

Wherever he went, people recognized him as "the moon-rocket man." There was little else in his life except his work. His mother had lived to see her son's fame for only seventeen days before she died on January 29, 1920. A year later his father remarried. Jennie Ward Messick, the new Mrs. Goddard, was a distant cousin and close friend of his mother's.

Robert Goddard was not a recluse. It was just that he found his work so interesting, it consumed much of his time. He loved music, played the piano well, and liked dancing. From time to time he escorted young women to parties and concerts. But he had had no special relationship since his engagement to Miriam Olmstead was broken twelve years before. When he returned to teaching after the war, he met the new secretary to the president of Clark University. Her name was Esther Kisk. Esther was seventeen years old; Robert Goddard was thirty-six. He learned that Esther was working to earn money to pay her way through college. The smitten professor disguised his wish to see her by asking if she would be interested in earning extra money by typing his notes and papers. Esther Kisk took on the additional work. Robert Goddard spent many evenings at her home translating his impossible-to-read penmanship. But when he asked her for a date, she said no. Sometimes he was able to persuade her to take drives in the country in his brand-new Oakland roadster. But Esther Kisk left Worcester in the fall of 1920 to enroll at Bates College in Lewiston, Maine, several hundred miles away.

Scientists in Europe became interested in Goddard's rocket work after reading newspaper accounts of his paper published by the Smithsonian. A few months later he received a letter from Robert Esnault-Pelterie, a French aviation pioneer who had written that a rocket motor

Esther C. Kisk in 1917.

could only be 3-percent efficient. He questioned the 64-percent efficiency Goddard claimed. Dr. Goddard sent him a copy of *A Method of Reaching Extreme Altitudes*, and they struck up a lively correspondence.

An astronomer at the Vatican wrote Goddard a letter of inquiry about his rocket. The Italians and Japanese asked for plans. The German consulate in New York requested copies of all his writings. The Germans in 1920 were discussing space travel publicly. In May 1922, he received a letter from Dr. Hermann Oberth of Romania and later Germany, who was also working on a rocket to go out of Earth's atmosphere. Oberth asked for a copy of

Goddard's extreme altitudes publication, too. Although he was uneasy about doing so, Goddard sent it to him. After reading it, Oberth offered to work with Goddard and scientists of other nations so they could share their information and develop a means of traveling to outer space. But Goddard wanted nothing to do with cooperative ventures; he worked alone.

The next year Oberth published a paper entitled *The Rocket into Planetary Space* and sent a copy to Goddard. In reading over this paper, Goddard was greatly disturbed that much of Oberth's work paralleled his own. Oberth claimed to have thought of the use of liquid hydrogen and oxygen in 1912; Goddard thought of it in 1909. Goddard wrote several papers comparing Oberth's work to his own as if to establish that he, Goddard, had done it first. Goddard asked that these papers be kept on file at the Smithsonian Institution and at Clark University. He did not want them made public yet. Most were not published until decades later.

He presented another paper, "On the Present Status of the High-altitude Rocket," at a meeting of the American Association for the Advancement of Science, in 1923, after Oberth's work was published. At the end of his paper, Goddard said, "This has been distinctly an American piece of work; it originated in America, as the writer's own interest and endeavors date back to 1899; the first theoretical work was published and the first experiments performed in America, and it seems very desirable that enough support be had to enable the work to be completed at an American laboratory." The next year, he restated these points in an article in the magazine *Nature* published in England; again, he showed that he had done his work before Oberth had done his.

Goddard dismissed Oberth's work as theoretical, while his own consisted of actual experiments toward construction of a working model. Yet despite these writings, which Oberth may have read, Oberth continued to send Goddard questions, and German magazines persisted in pestering him with requests for articles. Yet publicly the Germans said Goddard was too conservative. They cited his published denials about reaching the moon.

Conservative indeed. Several years earlier, in March 1920, Goddard had sent to the Smithsonian a report entitled, "Further Developments of the Rocket Method of Investigating Space." In this remarkable paper he talked about his long-held idea of taking photos of the moon and other planets. He had worked out how to track a rocket, adjust its inflight path, and bring it safely back to Earth using a heat shield and a parachute. He said liquid hydrogen and solid oxygen should be used instead of smokeless powders; they would have three times the energy and were cheaper. He also theorized about making hydrogen and oxygen using solar power on the moon or another planet since they were colder than Earth. Most astonishing for the times, he spoke seriously about piloted rockets: "The presence of an operator is desirable under many circumstances, for example, in place of an automatic camera, if a planet is encircled. An operator is essential if investigations are made that would necessitate landing on and departing from planets." In later additions to this report, he talked about possible inhabitants of other planets. But he would not allow the Smithsonian to publish this paper either. It was too soon to talk about people in space regardless of what the Germans said about his being too conservative.

The Smithsonian found his ideas all very interesting.

But they were becoming impatient to see a workable model of the high-altitude rocket for their four years of financial support. With all the newspaper fanfare surrounding the publishing of his high-altitude paper, Dr. Goddard was discouraged as well as embarrassed. It had been over twenty years since he had experienced his vision of a space vehicle while he sat in his grandmother's cherry tree. Since then he had worked with incredible single-minded purpose toward that goal. Once he wrote that "the whole problem is one of the most fascinating in the field of applied physics that could be imagined." He had worked out the theory that proved it could be done. But he still had no rocket that would head straight up into space. His military rockets were designed to go short distances horizontally.

With a part-time graduate assistant, Dr. Goddard set out one more time to make the multiple-charge vertical rocket work. The multiple-charge idea was something like the principle upon which a machine gun was based. That is, smokeless powders were packed into cartridges fixed to fire off in quick succession, each one giving the rocket an additional boost. Goddard and his assistant tried again and again. They even hoisted a rocket up fifty feet in the air and suspended it between two trees to give it a head start, but that trial, too, ended in the rocket crashing. A lot of little things went wrong. Some small part broke, burned up, or failed to function. They would fix that, and on the next test, some other little part failed. They moved the rocket's proving ground to "Aunt" Effie Ward's farm in Auburn, a drive of about five miles over dirt roads from Worcester. People near the Clark University campus were complaining about the noise of the rocket experiments. Goddard succeeded in getting one of these rockets to go up sixty feet before something went wrong and it crashed.

Yet somehow, Dr. Goddard was never discouraged by these failures. His philosophy was that he learned from them. He said, "It is not a simple matter to differentiate unsuccessful from successful experiments, since most work that is finally successful is the result of a series of unsuccessful tests in which difficulties are gradually eliminated."

But by January 1921 even Goddard had given up and made no more attempts with the multiple-charge rocket. He faced the hard fact that these explosion-type propellants were impossible to control. They could not give enough thrust to send the rocket where he wanted it to go. He had to turn to something else.

Back in 1909, Goddard had figured out in theory what an excellent propellant a mixture of liquid hydrogen and oxygen would be—hydrogen because of its great energy potential, and oxygen because it would be needed in the vacuum of outer space to make the hydrogen burn. Solid fuels like gunpowder and smokeless powders were fine for fireworks and short-range weapons, but space flight would require sustained power over a long period of time. Liquid fuels could be controlled. They could be turned off or reduced when not needed during flight.

Dr. Goddard theorized that the two liquids had to be fed into a combustion chamber by one of two methods: "[B]y allowing the two liquids to flow together slowly by gravity, and second, by forcing the liquids together under pressure." That was Goddard's theory. But in the real world, no liquid hydrogen existed outside small amounts in laboratories, and liquid oxygen had to be kept at -297°F to remain a pale blue liquid.

As a substitute for liquid hydrogen, Goddard reasoned he might use a cheap, readily available substitute—

ordinary gasoline. Gasoline was a combination of only two elements: hydrogen and carbon. Yet how could burning these two elements be possible? Gasoline, even gasoline vapors, was extremely explosive. As for oxygen, no one could light a flame in a room where it was in use. Goddard was warned not to do this, but he recognized the hazards and proceeded carefully.

Building parts and apparatus to use gasoline and liquid oxygen meant almost starting over. Liquid oxygen was so scarce that he had to travel to a laboratory at the Massachusetts Institute of Technology near Boston to get it. He carried it home in a Dewar flask, a vacuum bottle that could keep it cold and so prevent it from evaporating instantly. Later, he was able to buy liquid oxygen from the Linde Air Products Company at ten dollars for two liters, a high price to pay in 1920.

The work progressed slowly owing to a lack of funds. By the end of 1923, the new liquid-propellant rocket was "still in the testing-table stage." That year, he appealed for another $1,000 from Clark University; he did not get it. At the beginning of 1924, he again asked the Smithsonian Institution for aid and was granted $500. The American Association for the Advancement of Science gave him another $190. This forced Goddard to experiment on small-scale models weighing only a few pounds because liquid oxygen and parts were so expensive. The smallness of scale also hindered him because parts had to be made in miniature.

Goddard had to design and build special tanks and pipes to hold the liquid propellants. Before he could do this, he had to make tests with different kinds of metals and different thicknesses of each. Which ones would not get brittle and crack from the nearly -300°F liquid oxygen or would not burn through in the superheat of combustion? He had to find some way to feed just the right amount of the fuels into the combustion chamber. To obtain the 8,000-feet-per-second velocity he needed to lift a rocket against gravity, the gasoline and oxygen would have to burn at 5,000°F. But what kind of metal could he use? Aluminum melts at 1,250°F and nickel at 2,650°F. Iron becomes liquid at 2,763°F and boils at 5,432°F. He had to invent an igniter to get the fuels to start burning without causing an explosion. The proper nozzle needed to be designed for the gases from the combustion to escape while giving maximum efficiency and thrust without burning off. In making all these parts, he had to keep the weight of them to an absolute minimum, for the more the rocket weighed, the more fuel it would need to burn to lift off.

It was a series of trial-and-error tests, day in and day out, year in and year out. Not until October 1924 did Dr. Goddard have the individual parts working successfully enough to begin actually constructing a rocket. A year later Goddard tested the rocket in a testing frame—a device that holds the rocket and keeps it from flying away when its engines are turned on. The rocket lifted a distance of one foot for twenty-seven seconds until the fuel was used up. It had taken him five years, but the liquid propellants worked. Now he was ready for a flight test.

While Goddard was working so intently, Dr. Arthur G. Webster, who had been his teacher, mentor, friend, and boss, died suddenly. It was a great loss to Goddard personally as well as to Clark University.

Six months later, Dr. Robert H. Goddard was named head of the physics department in Webster's place. With this new position and increased salary, he felt he could afford to get married. Robert Goddard persuaded Esther Kisk to marry him, at last, over the objections of her family owing to their age difference and his uncertain health. The couple were wed at St. John's Episcopal Church in Worcester on June 21, 1924. After a week's honeymoon in the White Mountains of New Hampshire, they returned to live at Maple Hill. Grandmother Goddard had willed the house to her grandson when she died.

Although she had previously typed many notes and papers for Robert, Esther still had little idea about her husband's lifework. When he talked about discarding empty tanks during the rocket's ascent to allow faster acceleration, she didn't know what he was talking about. Or when he explained that he had figured out how to land

Professor Robert H. Goddard teaching a physics class at Clark University in 1924.

a rocket on the moon without jarring it and have it return to Earth, it was beyond her wildest imagination. But he had a job for his wife to do that would involve her with the rocket. Optimistically, he had purchased a French Sept motion-picture camera that ran seven seconds without rewinding so she could photograph his rocket test flights.

Late in February 1926, Goddard and his assistant, Henry Sachs, took the rocket to Aunt Effie's farm in Auburn for testing in the frozen farm fields. The rocket by now was 10½ feet long and weighed about 6 pounds empty and 10 pounds when loaded with gasoline and liquid oxygen. In its launching frame made out of pipe, the rocket did the usual balky things. Parts broke; pieces burned off. Other times they would wait all day in the cold New England winter only to have the weather be too windy to try an experiment.

On March 16, 1926, Goddard and Sachs went out to Auburn and set up the rocket in the morning. Knowing it took a long time, Esther Goddard and Professor Percy Roope from the physics department did not arrive until early afternoon to take photos—if there was anything to take. Goddard, always cautious because he knew better than anyone else the power of what he was working with, had built a protective sheet-iron shelter near the launch tower. At 2:30 in the afternoon, Esther Goddard and Percy Roope stepped behind the shield. Dr. Goddard turned the handle of the oxygen cylinder. His assistant used a blow-torch to heat an igniter filled with black powder. The heat from the igniter opened valves, and gasoline and liquid oxygen flowed into the combustion chamber. Henry Sachs used his blowtorch again to light an alcohol burner under the liquid oxygen tank to turn it from a liquid to a gas.

There was a short, loud bang, and a white-hot flame

Robert H. Goddard stands by the liquid oxygen-gasoline-fuel rocket in the frame from which it was fired on March 16, 1926, in Auburn, Massachusetts.

came out of the nozzle. From behind the shield, Goddard pulled the release cord that would free the rocket from the launching frame. Nothing happened. For almost a minute, the rocket roared, but did not move. Then it slowly started upward, clearing the 15-foot tower. It gained speed and altitude until it reached 41 feet. With its fuel used up, it arced over and kept on going until it crashed into the snow-covered field 184 feet away.

History was made in two and a half seconds. This was the world's first flight of a rocket using liquid propellants. Robert Goddard's theory and mathematical calculations had been right. Now, he thought, what remained was to build bigger and better rockets to go to upper altitudes, to the moon, to other planets, to outer space someday.

6

Little Nell and the Lone Eagle

After so many years, Dr. Goddard could not trust himself to believe what he had seen. He didn't say much; he was always the staid New Englander. The film in Esther Goddard's Sept camera had run out long before the rocket left the launch tower. There was no proof that this momentous occasion had occurred except the word of four eyewitnesses—and maybe a fifth, Aunt Effie, if she had happened to glance out her kitchen window. Goddard decided to repeat the test as soon as he could put the rocket back together again. Repeating the same experiment and getting the same results was the only way a theory could be proved scientifically.

After picking the rocket pieces out of the snow, he and Henry Sachs took them back to the laboratory at Clark University and put the rocket back into flying condition. Goddard added two rods to brace it and reduced the amount of precious liquid oxygen the rocket held. He also changed the location of the combustion chamber, positioning it below the gasoline and oxygen tanks instead of above them as had been the case on the successful rocket used March 16.

Back they all went to Aunt Effie's farm a week later. Robert Goddard and Henry Sachs set off the rocket. Esther Goddard took photos, and Percy Roope watched. The rocket rose out of the tower but landed only 50 feet away in a little over 4 seconds instead of 184 feet in 2½ seconds. Goddard's additions to the rocket had made it too heavy. Such was the delicate balance of the rocket.

When he wrote to Dr. Charles G. Abbot at the Smithsonian Institution about his success of March 16, Abbot congratulated him. But when Goddard wanted to make a bigger rocket, Dr. Abbot asked how much money he would need for a rocket large enough to reach a high altitude. Goddard replied that he thought he could do it in eight to twelve months for $6,500. In July 1926, the Smithsonian granted him the money, but for it the institution wanted a truly "spectacular" and useful flight.

Goddard set to work building a larger rocket that would carry twenty times the propellant of the previous version. The higher it was to go, the more propellant it would need. Yet this meant that once again he almost had to start over again. He said that "it is nevertheless impossible to make the larger rocket merely by increasing all the dimensions of the small rocket in the same ratio. Each part of the large rocket, planned in accordance with the results already obtained, must be tested and altered as found necessary, until it works properly in its relation to the whole."

For the next year, Goddard tested, altered, and tested

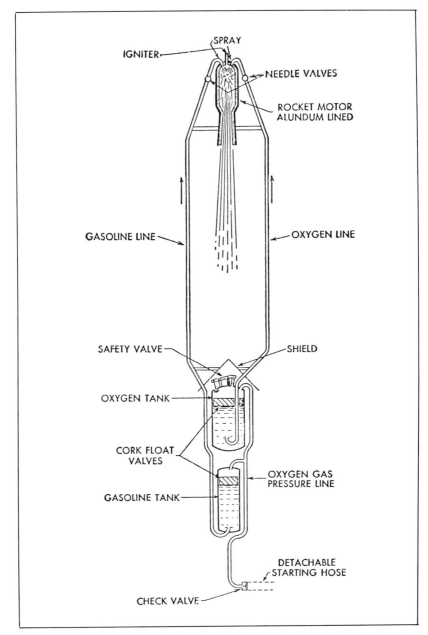

This drawing by Robert H. Goddard shows the cross section of his 1926 liquid-fuel rocket.

in his laboratory. In preparation for a flight test, he purchased from a farmer an old windmill tower used for pumping water and generating electricity. He had it dismantled and moved to Aunt Effie's farm. There he rebuilt, modified, and strengthened it to serve as a rocket launch tower sixty feet tall.

On May 3, 1927, according to the schedule he had promised the Smithsonian, he was ready to make the important test flight. After igniting the rocket, it moved up with a lifting force against gravity Goddard measured at over 200 pounds. He was delighted to see that the rocket was able to lift more than its own 150 pounds of loaded weight. Then the gas tank blew up.

By the middle of July, Goddard was ready to test again. He had added some improvements to prevent any more accidents. One such improvement was a way of stopping combustion so the gas tank wouldn't blow up again. His high hopes for a "spectacular flight" were the only things that were high. Certainly the rocket wasn't. For the rest of the summer, he tried test after test, but something always went wrong. By the beginning of September, he had to give up. The rocket was too big to fly. He decided to build another one only four times larger than the successful 1926 model. It was too great a leap between forty-one feet and "a spectacular flight."

Disturbing news kept filtering out of Europe. In 1927, some scientists formed the Verein für Raumschiffahrt (the German Society for Space Travel). They soon had 800 members. Alarms came from other sources. The American consul in Cologne, Germany, reported to the U.S. State Department that a German named Max Valier and the Opel Car Company had invented a rocket-propelled racing car. It had twelve rockets that pushed the car to speeds of seventy miles per hour. The State Department consulted the Smithsonian, which asked Robert Goddard what he knew about it. He said the car must be powered by black powder, which he had used in developing weapons for the U.S. Navy. Another German, Willy Ley, a member of the Verein für Raumschiffahrt, wrote to him saying he was doing a book on the history of rockets and space travel and needed to know what Goddard had done. Goddard replied that he had published nothing since the extreme altitude paper and hinted that he had done much more work but wouldn't tell Ley what it was.

In 1926 the Russian Konstantin Tsiolkovsky wrote a revised edition of his 1903 *Investigation of Space by Means of Rockets*. In it he mentioned the work of Goddard and Oberth as coming *after* his own. Tsiolkovsky's work was all theory. As far as it is known, unlike Goddard, he did few if any experiments.

These years were a sad time for Robert Goddard. His father was dying of throat cancer. Goddard went back to Roxbury and took pictures of his old home, the business his father had once owned, and other places where they had had happy family times long ago. He made the pictures into an album as a last Christmas present for Nahum Goddard, who died on September 15, 1928.

With the death of his father, Goddard was free to leave Worcester. He had a sabbatical leave of almost a year with pay coming from the university; he had been postponing it because of his father's illness. After the frustration of trying to do his tests in the unpredictable and often harsh New England weather, he thought about going West, maybe back to Pasadena and the California Institute of Technology. Some of the researchers there had become interested in his work, and he would be welcome.

Meanwhile, work went on with another $5,000 from the Smithsonian. On July 17, 1929, the institution got more than it had bargained for.

At 2 P.M., Goddard and his assistant ignited a 32-pound, 12-foot-long rocket and released it. With a loud roar and spouting a steady white flame, it rose to an altitude of 100 feet and landed 171 feet from the tower. Of course, something had to go wrong. In this case the parachute failed to deploy, and the gas tank exploded on impact with the ground. Parts of the device were scattered all over Aunt Effie's farm. But it was the first rocket to carry a scientific payload: a camera to take pictures and a barometer to measure air pressure. These instruments were still working when Goddard found them.

While Robert, Esther, and the research assistants hunted for the precious parts, they noticed ambulances, police cars, and fire trucks heading toward them. When the caravan reached the launch site, Goddard remained unconcerned and asked the police why they were there. It seemed neighbors had reported a fiery plane crash. Goddard realized someone had seen his flaming, high-flying rocket and had mistaken it for a plane. That was a natural mistake, since only Dr. Goddard and a few assistants had ever seen a rocket before. Goddard tried to jolly the police chief out of any concern. He explained that he was a professor at Clark University who was doing some small but maybe noisy experiments out on his aunt's farm, where he wouldn't bother anybody. It really wasn't worth mentioning to anyone. The police officer seemed to understand, but the reporters who had come along were busy looking at the charred grass and the burned rocks under the launch tower. They recognized Goddard as "the moon-rocket man" and began bombarding him with questions.

Robert and Esther Goddard and his assistants escaped. But once back in Worcester, Goddard immediately telephoned the editors of the newspapers to get them to kill the story. Too late, the newspapers were already out on the street. The stories contained exaggerations about how a rocket to the moon had blown up in midair. By the next day the story had been picked up by newspapers across the country including Washington, D.C. Dr. Charles G. Abbot of the Smithsonian fired off a telegram to Goddard asking just how successful had this rocket been with all the public attention.

People really believed a small rocket had been on its way to the moon. They ignored Goddard's statements that he had never intended such a thing. He had used a cup or two of gasoline and two or three cups of liquid oxygen. This amount of fuel could not have carried the rocket around a city block, much less some 230,000 miles to the moon. But in the Roaring Twenties, people were used to such outrageous stunts as pilots walking on the wings of flying airplanes at county fairs and grown men sitting on the tops of flagpoles or going over Niagara Falls in barrels. They were so used to flash and trash, they believed almost anything. Some stories about the rocket were so outrageous that one of Goddard's assistants named the rocket Little Nell after the much put-upon heroine of an old melodrama.

The newspaper stories stirred up the citizens around Auburn. They wanted the rocket tests outlawed as a public menace. The Massachusetts state fire marshal told Dr. Goddard that he could only test in a small area. Goddard knew future tests could not be limited as he was striving for longer and longer distances. The newspaper stories also brought hordes of sightseers and reporters, who swarmed all over the farm and waited for the next launch.

For Goddard, who liked secrecy about his work, this would never do. Besides, he was concerned someone could get hurt. Realizing that he must move his test site soon, he drove around the area near Worcester and found Camp Devens, an army rifle and artillery range. Since it was U.S. government property, the state of Massachusetts would have nothing to say about his tests. He appealed to the Smithsonian to get permission from the government for him to use it. Goddard took down his launch tower and shelter at Aunt Effie's farm, moved it to Devens, and erected it again. He turned a little target practice building riddled with shell holes into a shelter for himself and his assistants. It was drafty, but Goddard put an old stove in it for warmth. Nearby was a large shell hole filled with water. After the Goddard rocket team had been there a while, they named it Hell Pond and with good reason. Goddard never got a successful test over Hell Pond. The rocket would be in perfect working order leaving the laboratory at Clark University. By the time it was shaken and jostled on the dirt road into Devens, it refused to function.

On Friday afternoon, November 22, 1929, Dr. Goddard was in his office at Clark University when his telephone rang. He answered it, and the voice at the other end said, "This is Charles Lindbergh." It was the most famous man in the world.

Charles Lindbergh had captured the imagination of the world when he flew a single-engine plane solo 3,400 miles from New York City to Paris, France, in 33½ hours nonstop, on May 20–21, 1927. He was the first man to accomplish such a daring feat. Many before him had died trying. Man was almost a misnomer for Lindbergh. He was a twenty-five-year-old Minnesota "farm boy," who had

67

flown out of nowhere, a barnstorming pilot who gave flying exhibitions at county fairs and flew the mail. This clean-cut, young hero with the captivating smile had done something real in flying the Atlantic Ocean solo, not a stunt, and people loved him for it. They called him the Lone Eagle.

Lindbergh lived, ate, and slept flying. Until he flew the Atlantic Ocean and became famous, he had no other life. When he had conquered the sky, he looked toward outer space. Rockets crossed his mind as a way to get there. He even talked to engineers about it. But they were skeptical. Some said a combustion chamber would have to be lined with bricks in order not to burn through.

When Lindbergh saw a story about Robert Goddard in *Popular Science Monthly*, he checked with people he knew at the Massachusetts Institute of Technology. He learned that Goddard was head of the Clark University physics department. Lindbergh telephoned at once to ask for an appointment. The next day, he drove his Franklin car from New York City to Worcester.

Dr. Goddard showed his famous visitor around the laboratory, all the while discussing what he had accomplished. Lindbergh was amazed to see not one but several rockets that had flown when just a few weeks before he had been told by engineers and scientists that it could not be done. When Lindbergh mentioned their idea of a brick lining for a combustion chamber, Goddard showed him *his* combustion chamber made of the metal Duralumin 1/32 of an inch thick. Duralumin was made of aluminum, copper, manganese, and magnesium. It was very strong but lightweight. Goddard had proven already it could withstand the tremendous heat of burning hydrocarbons and liquid oxygen because he had devised a curtain cooling system. Gasoline was sprayed on the walls of the combustion chamber to cool it while the white-hot heat of actual combustion took place in the center of the chamber.

When he showed Lindbergh the films of the July 17 test, Lindbergh was convinced rocketry was worth pursuing. Like Goddard, Lindbergh looked far into the future and predicted how rocketry might advance aviation. He also could see clearly the here and now. Lindbergh asked Goddard how much he thought it would cost to carry on his research work full-time. Robert Goddard had dreamed about such funding for a long time. He knew just what to say—$100,000 over the next four years. Lindbergh promised to try to help him.

True to his word, four days later Lindbergh called Goddard. He said he had set up a meeting with Henry du Pont for 11 A.M. the next day in Wilmington, Delaware, the du Pont company's headquarters. Goddard scrambled to make the train.

At the meeting with Lindbergh, du Pont, and three du Pont laboratory scientists, Goddard discussed what he had done. But he became uneasy quickly. The scientists seemed determined to find out every last detail of his work. Goddard was just as determined they would not. By this time, he was a master at guarding his discoveries. Later, when he talked to Lindbergh alone, the flyer seemed to feel the same way Goddard did. Lindbergh wanted to see scientific research on the rocket, not just commercial uses. Goddard wrote later, "Lindbergh...impressed me very favorably throughout these events, and I believe he is a keen-minded young man."

On the way back from Wilmington to New York, Lindbergh gave Goddard his first plane ride. Lindbergh, the aviator, wanted to show Goddard, the rocket scientist, what a plane could do. He took it up to 6,000 feet and skimmed the treetops at 50 feet as the wind whistled past Goddard's ears in the open cockpit. Robert Goddard never forgot that ride.

By December 10, Lindbergh had arranged a meeting with John C. Merriam, president of the Carnegie Institution. Surrounded by other scientists and his friend Dr. Abbot of the Smithsonian, Goddard was much more talkative about his work. Lindbergh said that to further aviation, the rocket needed to be developed because propeller-driven planes only worked in the atmosphere and had probably already reached their maximum speed. These scientists were able to see the many uses of rockets in the future and the knowledge that could be gained by high-altitude research. The next week, the Carnegie Institution sent Goddard $5,000 for research, but it could not give him the full support he needed.

In January, Charles Lindbergh had to go to the West Coast on business. Except for a brief telegram in February, Goddard did not hear from him for months. By March, Goddard thought that Lindbergh had forgotten about him or lost interest in the rocket research.

But Lindbergh had not forgotten. He talked to financiers around the country. When he returned to New York in May, he called on Daniel Guggenheim, the father of his friend, Harry Guggenheim, who had been a naval aviator in World War I. Harry Guggenheim saw the great future aviation could have, but he also saw it needed help to reach its destiny. In 1926 he had persuaded his wealthy industrialist father to set up the Daniel and Florence Guggenheim Fund for the Promotion of Aeronautics with $3,000,000. The Guggenheim Fund established the first School of Aeronautics at New York University. By 1929, 1,400 young men were enrolled in aeronautical engineering courses in colleges across the country. The Guggenheims persuaded the brilliant Budapest-born scientist Dr. Theodor von Kármán to come from Germany to the United States and do research at the California Institute of Technology. (Kármán had been the director of the Aeronautical Institute in Germany from 1912 to 1930.) The Guggenheim Fund promoted flight safety and gave financial backing to start the airline industry. When Lindbergh met with Daniel Guggenheim at his mansion on Long Island, New York, he truthfully laid the pros and cons of Goddard's work before him. Trusting Lindbergh's judgment, Guggenheim promised him $25,000 a year for the next two years for Goddard's work, with a review of the work at the end of that time. The only promise he extracted from Lindbergh was that he would serve on an advisory board overseeing Goddard's work.

To administer this large amount of money, the Clark University Research Corporation for the Measurement and Investigation of High Altitudes was set up. Eight men were appointed to the advisory board besides Lindbergh. They included Dr. John C. Merriam, chairman of the committee and president of the Carnegie Institution; Dr. Charles G. Abbot of the Smithsonian; Dr. Walter S. Adams, director of the Mount Wilson Observatory; Dr. Wallace W. Atwood, president of Clark University; Colonel Henry Breckinridge, the lawyer for Daniel Guggenheim; Dr. John A. Fleming, also of the Carnegie Institution; Dr. C. F. Marvin, chief of the U.S. Weather Bureau; and Dr. Robert A. Millikan, director of the physics laboratories at the California Institute of Technology and winner of the Nobel Prize for Physics in 1923. These were some of the leading scientists of the day, and they believed in Robert

Goddard's work. He was no longer alone. In return for this financial support, Goddard promised to donate one half of any profits from his work to scientific research.

On July 10, 1930, Clark University released to the press a thorough history of Goddard's work and the future projects he hoped to accomplish under the Guggenheim grant. Clark University also stated what benefits this work would bring, such as charting atmospheric air temperatures, pressures, and winds, which would help aviation. Another goal was photography of the sun without the distortion of the atmosphere. The university said it hoped through Goddard's work it would be possible to study the effects of the electricity in the upper atmosphere on radio transmission. Again, Robert Goddard and his rocket were front-page news.

7

Westward Ho!

Dr. Goddard could now afford to go anywhere in the country. With the help of a professor of meteorology, he found that the best place for his work would be the high plains country of southeast New Mexico. He asked Henry Sachs, Albert Kisk (his brother-in-law), Larry and Charles Mansur, and their families to go with him.

They dismantled the old windmill launch tower at Camp Devens and crated up the equipment loaned to him from the Clark University machine shop—lathes, milling machines, and welders used to shape and cut metals to make parts. Along with the family furniture, it was all packed into a railroad boxcar and sent west.

On July 15, 1930, Robert and Esther Goddard got in their secondhand red Packard coupe and headed for Roswell, New Mexico. After a hard ten-day cross-country auto trip, the first thing that Dr. Goddard did when they reached Roswell was to visit the U.S. Weather Bureau station. Before he could make a final decision on where to settle, he had to go over years of climate records. He found that although the weather was free from subzero winters, it did have hundred-degree sizzling summers. But that didn't matter to Dr. Goddard. Heat or not, the weather would be good for rocket launching year-round. He looked at what else Roswell had to offer.

It was an old pioneer town of 11,000 people on the Rio Hondo, a tributary of the nearby Pecos River. Perhaps remembering the old frontier saying, "No law west of the Pecos," Dr. Goddard checked out the people, too. He had come west not only for the climate but also not to be bothered by reporters and curiosity seekers. New Mexico had come into the Union as the forty-seventh state in 1912, so the people of Roswell still lived by the code of the frontier; westerners did not ask questions of strangers. Every person's past was his or her own business. Just to lay to rest any doubts the townspeople might have had, Goddard gave a talk at the Rotary Club. He discussed his work in general terms so no one would think he was some "mad professor" conducting fiendish experiments when his rockets went off.

Roswell had two other important advantages. The Atchison, Topeka and Santa Fe Railroad stopped there, so Goddard could get his machinery and supplies. It was also home to many people with TB who had come for its warm, dry climate and pure air. The Goddards decided that this was the ideal place for them.

They set out house hunting and found Mescalero Ranch three miles northwest of town at the end of a dirt road. Goddard liked the privacy, and the ranch house was big enough for not only the Goddards to live in, but his assistants and their wives, too. They paid the owner $115-a-month rent and moved in.

Over the next few days, his assistants and the freight car with their furniture and equipment arrived. Sachs, Kisk, and the Mansur brothers set to work building a machine shop next to the house, while Goddard drove around the sparsely settled countryside looking for a flat launch site. He found one about ten miles from Mescalero. The rancher who owned it didn't even want the rent Goddard offered him. The place was called Eden Valley, and Goddard's assistants made a lot of jokes about their Nell moving from Hell Pond at Camp Devens to Eden Valley. Everyone hoped it meant the rocket would fly better.

As soon as the machine shop was built and equipped, the Goddard team moved the old windmill tower parts out to Eden Valley and reconstructed it. The lower twenty feet of the sixty-foot tower they covered with sheet iron to protect themselves and the delicate parts of the rocket from the sun, wind, and dust of the semidesert region. They built a control shed fifty-five feet away. It was a big improvement over the single piece of propped-up sheet iron they had used in Auburn.

When everything was in place, Goddard started his work. Although he was pressured to do something "spectacular" to please his financial backers, he refused to give in to the temptation of putting up a slapped-together, glorified Fourth of July Roman candle. He knew there could be no shortcuts to truly productive high-altitude flights that would expand scientific knowledge.

First, of course, he thought of theories or ways to solve problems; "doping it out" he called it. He often sketched out his plans on scraps of paper or the backs of envelopes before the ideas got away from him. Then he worked his ideas out mathematically. Next he or a draftsman drew up a formal set of plans that a machinist could follow to make a part. When it was completed, Dr. Goddard would test the part to see if it worked the way he originally planned. Each part had to undergo more changes until it did its large or small part in making the rocket fly.

Sometimes a part never would work, and Goddard would have to go back to his scraps of paper and design something else. He constantly had to go through the same process for even the smallest part because the tiniest misfit could keep the rocket grounded.

But before any rocket was taken out to the launch tower, it was put on a static frame Goddard had built outside the workshop at Mescalero Ranch. The rocket was held on the frame by weights and not allowed to fly when the fuels were ignited. Instead, it was hooked up to measuring devices to test the pounds of lift the burning fuel was giving and temperature gauges to check how hot and how efficiently the fuel burned. Only after many such tests had proved the parts were working would he wrap up the rocket and cart it out to the launching site for actual flight.

Even with all his careful work, once on the launch pad, the rocket would refuse to fly because some part did not function as planned and tested so many times. It was work that tried the patience of everyone. But Goddard never lost his. Instead, he would say that Nell needed a little fixing. As a true research scientist, he saw failures as opportunities to learn.

On December 22, 1930, after working at Roswell less than six months, Goddard and his men got Nell ready for a test at Eden Valley. This rocket was eleven feet long, nine inches in diameter, and weighed almost thirty-five pounds.

They hung it in the launch tower with cables, then loaded in the gasoline and precious liquid oxygen. After working all morning and part of the afternoon, they hoped the rocket was ready to soar. They retreated to the second control shelter they had built a thousand feet away. When the rocket was ignited and shot a steady flame out of its base and the gauges confirmed that the pressures were high enough, they pulled free the ten cables holding the rocket earthbound. The rocket, instead of soaring, got caught on the launch tower. Fortunately, the rocket was undamaged.

On December 30, they tried again, going through the hours of careful preparation. This time the motion-picture camera recorded the rocket soaring 2,000 feet above its launch tower, going 500 miles an hour. It had reached almost the speed of sound before it arced over and hit the ground 4,000 feet from the tower. Of course, one thing, at least, had to fail. The parachute Esther Goddard had sewed and stuffed into the nose cone did not deploy, so the rocket was bashed-in a little.

No one could say that Dr. Goddard was thrilled with success; he had not been in the West long enough to learn to whoop and holler. But everyone knew he was pleased when he said that the flight had been "interesting." The parts he had been working on—a pressure regulator using compressed gas to force the fuels into the combustion chamber—had worked, giving high efficiency to the fuel's burning. But that would need improving for higher altitudes; it was too heavy. The four lightweight Duralumin vanes he had added at the base of the rocket to act as rudders had given stability. But he could see that the rocket needed more stabilization to cause it to go straight up. He immediately set to work on developing automatic lightweight gyrostabilizers. On a rocket, a gyrostabilizer is more than just a little rotor wheel going around. Since it is encased in the rocket, something must get the gyroscope rotor started turning. Once it is, the gyroscope alone cannot steady the rocket. The vanes at the base of the rocket do that. Some means of controlling the guiding vanes by the gyroscope had to be devised. This can be done by gas pressure, electricity, or even magnets.

In the December tests, Dr. Goddard had been lucky. The combustion chamber had not burned through. But he had to find a way to make sure it *never* burned through by improving his curtain cooling system—or finding another way to do the job.

Goddard also learned from his otherwise unsuccessful test of December 22 that using three men to handle ten control cables required over a minute to start the rocket. That was too long, too complicated, and too dangerous. Among his next projects was one to devise a remote control using only one key that would fire the rocket and let it fly in a few seconds. He set about "doping" all these problems out.

Goddard thought that this test had proved he was making rapid progress on his work under the Guggenheim grant now that he could work full-time on it with the help of four assistants. He wrote a letter to Dr. John C. Merriam, the chairman of the advisory committee, requesting a meeting to show the committee what he had accomplished.

On February 20, 1931, seven of the nine board members, including Dr. Charles G. Abbot and Charles Lindbergh, met and viewed Esther Goddard's motion pictures of the December 30 test. They were fascinated and promised continued funding for the next year. That was the assurance Dr. Goddard had come to Washington for, once he had a successful flight. His benefactor and patron, Daniel Guggenheim, had died of a heart attack in September. The Guggenheim Foundation carried on its work under the guidance of his widow, Florence, and his son Harry. But the high-flying 1920s had crashed with the stock market in October 1929. This brought on the Great Depression that had grown worse and worse each year. In the United States 15 million people were out of work. They stood in bread lines and soup kitchens to get food just to stay alive.

Under these circumstances, Goddard was greatly relieved when he was given funds for another year. He went back to Roswell and back to work. Goddard knew he had to accomplish as much as possible because he had a feeling his funding might not continue all four years, especially now that the country was in serious economic trouble.

Goddard did not make any more flight tests until September and October 1931. Two flights reached 1,700 feet. In April 1932 he used his first gyroscope-controlled rocket. It rose, but not far. In another test a month later, just about everything went wrong. Goddard wanted these rockets to fly because his backers wanted to see results. Not that he had not accomplished much, he had. But the time it took to perfect the different parts of the rocket so they would do the things he theorized they could do was hard for outsiders, even other scientists, to understand. He decided to request another meeting of the advisory board and explain just what was happening in New Mexico. The meeting was arranged for May 24, 1932, in Washington, D.C. Only four members were present. His strongest supporter, Charles Lindbergh, was absent.

Ever since his solo flight over the Atlantic, Charles

Lindbergh and later his family had been front-page news. It seemed as if they were the target of every opportunist and outright nut living. On March 1, 1932, his two-year-old son was kidnapped out of his crib. For two and a half months, Lindbergh and his wife were tormented by ransom notes, crank calls, and letters by the thousands. Lindbergh devoted every moment to the search for his son. On May 12, the baby was found buried in a shallow grave on the Lindbergh property. The grieving Lindbergh could not attend the meeting with Goddard in Washington to give his support.

The four members of the advisory board at the meeting, Dr. John C. Merriam, Dr. Charles G. Abbot, Dr. Wallace W. Atwood, and Dr. John A. Fleming, listened carefully as Goddard described the work he had accomplished in the last year. His system of remote controls and pressure feeding of fuels had been successfully tested in flight. The burning efficiency had been steadily increased for maximum lift force with minimum weight. As a result, he had plans for testing a larger rocket that could carry more fuel and thereby reach higher altitudes. He was still working on perfecting the stabilization with gyroscopes.

The members of the committee were impressed and recommended to the Guggenheim Foundation that Goddard's work be supported for another two years. But Harry Guggenheim had to refuse the recommendation. The fall of the stock market and bank failures caused by the depression had shrunk the assets of the foundation. It could no longer support Goddard's work, at least not for the coming year.

Dr. Goddard returned to Roswell with a heavy heart. He deeply regretted having to lay off his faithful assistants in the depths of the Great Depression, but they understood there was nothing else he could do. They stored his equipment and crated his furniture. The old windmill launch tower stayed at Eden Valley; after all, it was not welcome in the state of Massachusetts. The last thing Dr. Goddard did was to place the ten-gallon hat he had bought when he came to Roswell on his desk in the machine shop. He hoped some day he would wear it again.

In October 1932, Robert Goddard celebrated his fiftieth birthday—a milestone that confounded and amazed his doctors. Every October 19 when he was in Worcester, he visited the old cherry tree behind his home at Maple Hill where he had his vision of a space vehicle as a boy. He called it the "anniversary." In over thirty years, no matter how discouraging his rocket work went—certainly no more discouraging than in 1932—Goddard never thought of any other way of life than pursuing his dream. He also reread H. G. Wells's *The War of the Worlds* and wrote a letter to Wells in England telling him of his appreciation of his book and how it had inspired him in his lifework.

With money no longer coming in from the Guggenheim Foundation, Dr. Charles G. Abbot of the Smithsonian sent him $250 to pay a part-time machinist. Goddard hired his brother-in-law, Albert Kisk. There was no thought of flight testing, for Goddard knew there would be no funds in the foreseeable future. They kept on working at improving small parts for the rocket. Goddard worked on heat insulators, experimented with lightweight welded and bolted joints, and continued work with stabilizing gyroscopes. He developed a way to turn the gasoline and liquid oxygen off and on quickly by pressure controlled valves. This work resulted in fourteen patents. One was for a combustion chamber with an outside cooling jacket that forced gasoline in through small holes in the walls of the chamber.

Another patent was for a "Propulsion Apparatus."

This was a rocket engine to be used in the atmosphere. Air taken in at the front of the engine would ram open shutters, or flappers, and mix with the fuel ignited by a spark. The explosion of the fuel would force the shutters closed for a moment. This gave short, rapid bursts, or explosions, of energy, up to 600 per second, that were then exhausted out of a nozzle or jet at the rear of the engine. Just as with the rubber balloon demonstration, described in Chapter 3, the reaction inside the engine gave a thrust, or forward force. Not having to carry its own air supply would allow the engine to be comparatively light. Goddard thought it could work on airplanes and give them greater speed than propellers alone could do. It was different from a rocket motor, which carried its own oxygen as well as fuel and could travel in the vacuum of outer space. Goddard called it a resonance chamber. Later it was known as a jet engine. The principle by which this engine worked came to be known as jet propulsion. The Germans bought that patent.

Up through the 1930s, the U.S. Patent Office sold plans to whomever asked for them. Goddard's original 1914 patents on the use of liquid and solid propellants and multistage rockets were running out. They were only good for seventeen years. Then anyone could make or sell the invention without permission or paying royalties. Goddard pleaded with the Patent Office to renew his patents in the interest of national defense. But the Patent Office ignored his pleas.

Goddard was increasingly bombarded with requests for plans and details about his work not only from Germany, but also from Japan and Italy. His standard answer to all such inquiries was to refer them to his 1920 paper on extreme altitudes. He usually added, "Much of my recent research on rockets is incomplete and has not yet been published, since the work has been discontinued, owing to the depression." He rejected any idea of cooperation with foreign researchers such as Hermann Oberth had once suggested. He felt he was the front-runner. To cooperate with anyone else would only help them, not him.

When the American Interplanetary Society, later called the American Rocket Society, was formed in 1930, it sent Goddard an honorary membership. Recognizing him as the world's leading authority on rockets, it asked him to give a speech at one of its meetings and become a permanent member of its advisory committee. Goddard accepted the honorary membership but politely turned down the advisory board position and the invitation to speak. He gave his standard excuse that his work was too incomplete to talk about yet. Goddard and his assistants, even with the generous help from the Guggenheim Fund, made rockets by hand in secrecy and patented everything. Yet much of what he did was acquired by foreign governments without giving him credit. He was therefore leery about sharing his information with anyone, even fellow American scientists.

In Germany, many scientists worked on making different parts of rockets. By 1931 they had a liquid-fueled engine with a thrust force of 110 pounds. They made eighty-seven tests with these rockets they called the Repulsors. Some went as high as 3,000 feet and landed safely with a parachute. (That same year, the Russians reached the same level of development.)

Germany had suffered a crushing and humiliating defeat in World War I. It had to give up its colonies in Africa and in the Pacific region and much of the land it had held in Europe for years. The German people revolted, overthrew their emperor, Kaiser Wilhelm II, and formed the Weimar Republic. But the republic was weak and the Germans were not used to democracy. When hard economic times hit Germany in the 1920s and early 1930s, the people voted for the Nazi political party headed by Adolf Hitler, who promised to rebuild the German economy. By 1934, Hitler was firmly in control as dictator of Nazi Germany. As "Der Führer," or leader of Germany, he began to build a powerful war machine with the intention of taking back land Germany had once held—and more.

The German army took over rocket development. The Germans fired two liquid-fueled rockets that went up over a mile. In 1937, they moved the work from Kummersdorf near Berlin to the secret location of Peenemünde by the Baltic Sea. Hundreds of engineers and scientists worked there on creating a far-ranging rocket that Hitler planned to use as a *wunder-waffen*—a "wonder weapon."

Rumors of the Germans' work reached people like Dr. Charles G. Abbot and Charles Lindbergh. Along with Harry Guggenheim, they urged Goddard to take his rocket research and plans to the U.S. military in hopes of getting funds from the army or navy to further his work. Armed with a letter of introduction from Dr. Abbot to the secretary of the navy, Goddard went to Washington in June 1933 and talked with several admirals about his rockets. He suggested that they could be used as antiaircraft weapons. Again, the Department of the Navy was not interested, saying that rockets would require too much expensive development with little chance for success. Thus the United States threw away the leading edge it had through Goddard's pioneer work in rocket weapons and jet propulsion.

A year after Goddard returned to Worcester, he decided to ask the Guggenheim Foundation about the possibility of funding his research again. But first he wrote to Charles Lindbergh emphasizing the military and aviation applications of his work even if the army and navy were not interested. He hoped that Lindbergh would intercede again for him with the Guggenheims. Goddard also contacted the Smithsonian about funding, but with the depression growing worse, the Smithsonian could give him no promises of money.

When he did not hear from Lindbergh, Goddard wrote directly to Harry Guggenheim about support for his work for another year, possibly two years as he had been originally promised. Guggenheim replied that his mother could not give $25,000 but would be willing to give $2,500 toward another year's work at Clark University.

Finally in July 1934, the Guggenheim Foundation gave him a one-year grant of $18,000 for *successful* full-flight experimentation. Immediately, Goddard requested a leave of absence from Clark University. By September 13, he had crated his furniture for shipment and driven cross-country to Roswell again. Opening up his shop at Mescalero Ranch, he picked up his ten-gallon hat off his desk and put it on his head.

8

Higher and Higher, Faster and Faster

The Goddards were back at Mescalero Ranch only two days when Charles Lindbergh and his wife, Anne, flew in to visit them. Esther Goddard could not even offer them dinner; she had not unpacked enough pans and dishes. The Lindberghs protested that they only planned to stay an hour; they were on their way home from California. But Charles Lindbergh became so interested in talking to Robert Goddard that the famous couple stayed until the next day. Before they left, Lindbergh took Robert and Esther Goddard for plane rides. Remembering his harrowing first ride with Lindbergh over Delaware, Dr. Goddard was not too keen on the idea of going up again. But he was in no position to refuse the world's foremost pilot. On the other hand, Esther Goddard found she loved flying and planned to learn how some day. Two days after the Lindberghs left Mescalero Ranch, the kidnapper of their baby was captured.

With amazing speed, Dr. Goddard and his assistants set up the shop again and repaired the old launch tower. Now that he could devote full time to his research, Goddard planned to build a series of larger rockets that would be between thirteen and fifteen feet long and weigh fifty-eight to eighty-five pounds empty. They would contain the improvements he had worked out during the two years he was back at Clark University. Among them were a new remote-controlled igniter he had patented and a light-weight gyrostabilizer. These larger rockets would look much different from his open, smaller models, in which he could see the liquid oxygen and gasoline chambers, the combustion chamber, and the piping that connected them. The new models would be streamlined, with cone-shaped heads, cylindrical sides made of shiny aluminum, and a flared bottom surrounding the nozzles. They would look strangely similar to the cylinders described by H. G. Wells in *The War of the Worlds*.

Following his standard procedure, Dr. Goddard did many tests in the static frame, then took the rocket to Eden Valley for a series of flight tests. During the first test, on February 16, 1935, the rocket left the tower headed straight up. Goddard estimated it had a strength of two *g*s. (One *g* is the acceleration against gravity—about thirty-two feet per second per second.) He was delighted, even though the combustion chamber burned through again in midair. As the rocket nosed over, the parachute deployed, but it was too small to gently lower the rocket to the ground. The delicate gyrostabilizer was badly damaged.

By March 28 the gyrostabilizer was repaired and installed on the rocket again. It was meant to stabilize the rocket so it would not arc over as it left the tower and would continue climbing until the fuel ran out and pro-

pulsion stopped. Then the gyrostabilizer would stop working, and the rocket would go into free flight as it returned
to earth. On the test, as the rocket shot skyward from the
tower, it wobbled from left to right to left but finally
steadied out to reach 4,800 feet before turning over and
traveling at the speed of sound (about 750 miles per hour)
and crashing two miles away. The rocket arced over because the center of its gravity changed as its fuel was used
up, making it unstable. But the gyrostabilizer had done its
job on the vertical part of the flight. A May 31 flight
reached an altitude of 7,500 feet, and on July 12, a flight
reached 6,000 feet.

With this string of successes, Goddard invited Lindbergh and Guggenheim to come to Roswell to see the
rocket fly for themselves. Finally, on September 22, 1935,
they arrived. Realizing only too well that further financial
backing for his work depended on good tests, Goddard
prepared not one but two rockets. On the first day he
showed his important visitors the shop, the two flight
models, and how he performed his static tests. The next
day dawned bright and fair, ideal testing weather. The
Goddards and their guests headed for Eden Valley at six in
the morning. At nine, with everyone safely behind the
shelters, Goddard pushed the lever to start the igniter. But
the igniter failed, and the rocket sat there in the launch
tower. Disappointed, but not surprised, Goddard readied
the second rocket for launching.

Two days later, they all went out to the valley again.
This time the rocket ignited, and a white flame shot out of
the bottom. It roared but did not rise, and the combustion
chamber soon burned through. Goddard was embarrassed. But Harry Guggenheim and Charles Lindbergh
were understanding. Even if Nell didn't fly, Harry Guggen-

This group photograph taken in 1935 at the Eden Valley rocket launching tower shows, from left to right, A. W. Kisk, Harry Guggenheim, Robert H. Goddard, Charles A. Lindbergh, and N. T. Ljungquist.

heim seemed impressed with Dr. Goddard's organization and approach to the problem of rocket flight in general. Lindbergh said that he thought Goddard had been successful so far and in time would accomplish what he planned to do.

It was unfortunate that Guggenheim and Lindbergh did not see a flight. Just about anyone whoever witnessed a successful rocket takeoff was overcome with emotion and turned into a believer. Even a small rocket was awesome. As it was, Guggenheim had seen enough to continue funding Goddard's work.

Even though these two rockets didn't fly, Lindbergh and Guggenheim thought it was important for Goddard to publish his recent work. They also thought it would be a good idea for him to send one of his rockets to the Smithsonian Institution so that his world lead in rocketry would be a matter of record. Reluctantly, Goddard agreed. A brightly polished rocket model was carefully packed into a box by Goddard's assistants and put on a train in Roswell. Esther and Robert Goddard watched sadly as the train pulled out of the station. It was as if they were seeing a beloved child off. When the rocket reached the Smithsonian, it was not put on display. Instead, it was stored behind a false wall. Dr. Goddard had given strict instructions when he consented to send the rocket to Washington: "It is understood that this is not to be placed on exhibition until requested by me, or in the event of my death, by Mr. Harry F. Guggenheim and Colonel Charles A. Lindbergh." On March 16, 1936, Robert Goddard's paper was published by the Smithsonian Institution under the title "Liquid Propellant Rocket Development." It was ten pages long, with an additional eighteen pages of pictures and drawings. It covered Goddard's work from 1930 to 1935 and described the results of his experiments.

As the paper was being prepared, several strange things happened. Goddard's mail was opened on its way to him. When the Smithsonian sent him a proof copy of his paper so that he could correct it before it was published, the paper never reached him in Roswell; it completely disappeared. Goddard was constantly bombarded year in and year out with requests from foreign governments for detailed information about his work. Again, he suspected espionage.

At Guggenheim and Lindbergh's urging to get his advances in rocket research recognized, Goddard reported on his work at a meeting of the American Association for the Advancement of Science in St. Louis, Missouri, on December 31, 1935. The title of his talk was "Progress in the Development of Atmospheric Sounding Rockets." It covered much the same points his liquid propellant paper did.

Goddard explained that his present rocket was twelve feet long, nine inches in diameter, weighed eighty pounds, and carried sixty pounds of fuel consisting of ordinary gasoline and liquid oxygen. These two fuels were fed in a continuous flow into the combustion chamber by pressure from compressed nitrogen gas. The rocket flew vertically, stabilized by a small gyroscope. The scientists present were speechless when he showed them his motion pictures of the rocket flights.

Goddard went on to tell them he needed to find a way to build a larger rocket that could carry more fuel and yet be lighter in weight. While his rocket could go faster than the speed of sound now, it would have to go many times faster to escape Earth's gravity. This was the problem he still had to solve.

The much larger rocket Dr. Goddard told the scientists about would weigh over 200 pounds and be four or five times the size of the one he had had so much success with in 1935. Instead of using nitrogen gas, he planned to use liquid nitrogen to pressure the liquid oxygen and gasoline into the combustion tank. For liquid nitrogen, he would need a much smaller and, therefore, lighter tank. Between November 1935 and February 1936, he did ten tests of a new, larger motor in the static frame. He said that "the greater the thrust for a chamber of a given weight, the greater the possible fuel load, and consequently the greater the height that can be reached."

In May, Goddard began to ready the rocket for a flight test. But the combustion chambers kept burning through. He even tried using four smaller motors instead of one large one. The rocket rose from the tower but went no place. By January 1937 he had to face the fact the larger rocket would not fly because the larger combustion chamber could not be effectively cooled. Yet he did not have time to redesign and test a new curtain cooling mechanism. He returned to flight testing a smaller combustion chamber model to obtain high flights as soon as possible. By reducing the diameter of the rocket from eighteen inches to nine inches, the new rocket weighed only about 100 pounds. This weight reduction allowed Goddard to double the amount of fuel he could load. He hoped this modification would increase the height the rocket could reach.

On March 26, 1937, the new rocket powered up quickly. When Goddard pressed the release switch freeing it to fly, it went up and up to an altitude between 8,000 and 9,000 feet. It went so high, the ground instruments lost sight of it in the haze. It stayed aloft 22.3 seconds—until the fuel was used up—then it arced over. The parachute deployed, but tore off, and the rocket landed 2,000 feet from the launch tower. The beautiful rocket was dented, but Goddard didn't care. What were a few dents when the rocket had flown the highest ever.

In late May, Robert and Esther Goddard went back to Worcester for the fiftieth anniversary celebration of Clark University. At the commencement ceremonies on June 5, usually dull affairs for the faculty who sit through them year after year, Goddard was jarred out of his state of bored inattention when Dr. Wallace W. Atwood, president of the university, began reading a letter from Charles Lindbergh. Lindbergh praised the work Goddard had done and drew a dramatic picture of the future of the rocket for science, for war, for commerce, and for explora-

A rocket launched from Eden Valley in 1937. It used gyrostabilizer steering.

tion of the universe. When President Atwood finished the letter, everyone gave Dr. Robert H. Goddard a standing ovation. Unfortunately, Goddard's great pleasure over this tribute to his work was marred when the newspapers put the "moon-rocket man" on the front page again.

When Goddard returned to Roswell, he worked even harder. His four machinists put in overtime. He often got up at three or four o'clock in the morning on a flight-testing day, worked until dark, and then spent the evening figuring and designing new parts. He did the opposite of what he should have been doing—resting—for his TB had flared up again, and he was frequently ill.

Charles Lindbergh kept up a correspondence with Goddard even though he had lived in England since 1935. The six-week trial of his baby's kidnapper had been sensational news all over the world. Even after it was over, the family was harassed constantly by the press until Lindbergh could no longer live in his own country.

After reading Goddard's reports on the success of his rocket, Lindbergh suggested he contact the National Aeronautic Association (NAA) in Washington, D.C. The NAA could send someone to record and verify the rocket flights to prove Goddard's lead in the world. Goddard agreed. Official high flights would have the best chance to get him financing in the cash-poor depths of the Great Depression that still gripped the country. Robert Goddard knew he was ahead of other researchers around the world. Although the Germans were making wild claims, for example, that they had put a twenty-four-foot manned rocket up six miles, these claims were never verified. For publicity, the Germans made many promises about what their rockets could do but never proved it in verifiable tests.

Lindbergh made several trips to Germany from 1936

to 1939 to learn about the air force the Germans were building. He made these trips to report back to the U.S. government. The Germans were delighted he was there. They tried to impress him with the might of their Luftwaffe, as they called their air force. Through Lindbergh, they sought to intimidate the rest of Europe into letting them take whatever land they wanted without putting up a fight. However, the top German officers were very secretive about whatever they were doing with rockets. Even Lindbergh could not find out. Goddard stressed in his letters to the NAA that whatever happened on his flights must remain a secret.

Three military observers from the nearby New Mexico Military Institute were appointed by the NAA to officially observe and record Goddard's flights. Goddard planned a test for June 16 in the late afternoon. But at 3:15 that day a tornado struck Eden Valley. The launch tower was torn from its concrete moorings and toppled to the ground in a broken, twisted heap with the rocket still inside. Fortu-

The collapsed rocket tower after a severe storm struck Eden Valley in 1938.

nately, Goddard's test rocket was not seriously damaged.

Goddard and his men dismantled the tower in the 100-degree desert summer heat. They took it back to the shop for rewelding and assembly. In a remarkably short time, the NAA tests were rescheduled for late July. Weather conditions caused postponements until August 9. The officers installed an official barograph from the U.S. Bureau of Standards on the rocket. A barograph is a recording barometer. By recording air pressure, such a device could be used to measure and make a record of the height the rocket could reach. Goddard feared that the barograph might be too heavy. He had learned from sad experience that the slightest extra weight could throw the delicately balanced lift force off, and the rocket would refuse to rise. Although Robert Goddard always appeared unaffected whether Nell was a success or failure, he admitted that despite checks and rechecks, there were many chances for error. He remarked that "my heart is in my mouth before every flight test we make." This time the rocket put on a perfect performance. It rose 6,565 feet, going almost straight up, its gyrostabilizers working. When the fuel ran out, the parachute opened, and the rocket returned to earth 0.4 of a mile from the tower, just as Goddard had designed it to do, and as it so often had not. This time the height reached was on official records.

After the exhausting work of rebuilding the tower and the exciting performance of the rocket, Dr. Goddard's health was worse. His wife persuaded him that he needed a vacation. War clouds were gathering around the world. Japan had invaded China. Italy had conquered Ethiopia. Germany had marched into Austria. The Goddards decided to see Europe before it blew up. On August 17, 1938, they sailed from New York on the French liner *Normandie*.

They visited France, Switzerland, and England, but Dr. Goddard refused to go near Germany.

When they returned to New York in September, the Goddards were invited to Harry Guggenheim's magnificent home on Long Island. Guggenheim made the suggestion that to speed up the work on a large rocket, Goddard should get others to work on the development of individual parts. Guggenheim even called up various manufacturers on the telephone to see what they could do to help. He also arranged a meeting between Goddard and Dr. Theodor von Kármán, director of the Daniel Guggenheim Aeronautics Laboratory and Dr. Robert Millikan, director of the physics laboratory, at the California Institute of Technology, to get their cooperation. But Goddard was unwilling to give away twenty-five years of solitary work. He dismissed the California Institute of Technology's research as being of no help to him because it was not working with liquid propellants. Reports from companies and other universities said that to develop any parts would take too much time and cost too much money.

Practical suggestions came from Major James H. Doolittle, the famous World War I ace pilot who now worked for Shell Petroleum Corporation. At Guggenheim's suggestion, he traveled to Roswell to meet Robert Goddard. After seeing the rocket, Doolittle offered to develop a high-efficiency fuel to replace the gasoline Goddard had been using. He saw that for the rocket to fly to high altitudes, the fuel must give the biggest bang per pound possible. It would simplify and lighten the rocket by eliminating the need for the nitrogen pressure system because the new fuel would have its own vapor pressure. This was the help Goddard needed from a man that understood flight, and he came along at the right time.

To make possible the rocket flight he had always envisioned, Goddard saw three major steps as necessary. The first was to develop a combustion chamber for controlled firing of liquid fuels. He had done that successfully. The second step was automatic stabilization to achieve almost vertical flight. He had accomplished that with the gyrostabilizer and retractable steering vanes at the base of the rocket.

The third step was to develop fuel pumps. He said, "I feel that there is no shortcut to high flights, and that work should be concentrated on pumps until a satisfactory pumping system had been made....The development most urgently needed was a small, lightweight fuel pump, capable of pumping either liquid oxygen or gasoline at high pressures." For short flights, pumps were not needed. Pressure feeding of fuels was enough. But for the high altitudes Goddard was aiming for, only pumps could supply the fuels fast enough and long enough to give the longest combustion time and greatest power. They would also be much lighter than the pressure tanks. The lighter the rocket's parts, the more fuel it could carry, the higher it would go—theoretically. Back at Clark during the years from 1932 through 1934, he had begun designing a centrifugal pump that, once it started, would continue to feed the fuels into the combustion chamber. He needed one pump for each fuel. Once he had the pumps, Goddard had to find a way to get them started and keep them going in flight.

He turned to the idea of turbines for a miniature power plant. A turbine is a wheel turned at high speeds by the force of moving water or gas. Turbines have blades that water or gas push against. A waterwheel was an old form of turbine. A windmill was another type of simple turbine turned by a gas—the air. Goddard devised an internal combustion boiler to change some of the liquid oxygen into a hot gas to drive the tiny turbine blades that ran the pumps to feed the liquid oxygen and fuel into the combustion chamber. He had it all worked out in theory, but it took much of 1938, all of 1939, and part of 1940 before his pumping system and the power plant to operate it were perfected enough to produce flight. The problems to be overcome were the most difficult so far in his work with rockets.

On August 1, 1940, Goddard had a rocket ready for a flight test. The flight didn't start out right, and he had to shut it down. After examining all the controls, he found no reason for the malfunction. On August 9, he tried again. The rocket ignited, was released, and slowly rose to an altitude of 300 feet. But it only rose at 10 to 15 miles an hour; then it started to tilt. The stabilizers did not function to straighten the rocket out, and it headed into the ground. Goddard found, after examining the parts, both fuel tanks had burst and ignited. But he was pleased anyway. He said, "Even though the flight was short, it demonstrated that the pumps, turbines and gas generator on the rocket operated in flight."

Flight testing was expensive because the rocket always sustained some damage. With war preparations going on, materials Goddard needed were becoming hard to get. He went back to testing in the static frame, where the whole rocket would not be damaged.

It wasn't until May 1941 that he tried another flight test using the pumps. Nell rose straight up 250 feet out of the tower before curving over. At least the parachute deployed. But it was Nell's last flight.

This rocket was 22 feet long, 18 inches in diameter,

Goddard's rocket in the launching tower, ready for its August 1940 test.

and weighed close to 500 pounds when loaded with fuel. Nell had grown since the days of its infancy in 1926, when it was 10½ feet long and weighed 5 pounds empty.

Goddard had his assistants clean and polish the rocket and put it in a wooden box for storage. His dream was not "down," but he would have no more time to work on it for a long while.

9

The War Years

On September 1, 1939, Germany invaded Poland. Two days later, Britain and France declared war on Germany, and World War II was on. As in 1914, when World War I started, the United States did not directly involve itself, but it did begin a program of preparedness. President Franklin D. Roosevelt requested that the nation's top scientists to form the National Defense Research Committee. He wanted them to advise him and put forward any scientific inventions or discoveries that could result in new and better military weapons in a hurry. The committee's chairman was Dr. Vannevar Bush, an electrical engineer and professor, dean of engineering, and vice-president of the Massachusetts Institute of Technology and from 1939 the president of the Carnegie Institution. The subcommittee on rocket propulsion was not chaired by Dr. Robert Goddard of Clark University. It was headed by Dr. Richard

C. Tolman, a physicist, professor, and (beginning in 1935) the dean of the Graduate School of the California Institute of Technology.

Unfortunately, Goddard had gained a reputation among his fellow scientists for secrecy. What really annoyed them was that he patented everything. In a war, things had to be done fast, and teamwork was the only way to do it. Dr. Goddard was not thought of as a team player. As a result, other scientists left him behind.

Back in 1938 Charles Lindbergh had suggested to Goddard that liquid-propelled rockets would have several important military uses. Dr. Goddard, having dealt with the military from 1917 to 1924, wrote back that "military men dislike calling on civilians for assistance, and particularly the making of appropriations to civilians. Also, there is strong skepticism among military men regarding such a new development as this."

Nevertheless, with the preparedness effort gaining momentum, Harry Guggenheim wanted to offer the government the rocket technology Goddard had developed as well as the facilities at Roswell. He arranged a meeting with General Henry H. ("Hap") Arnold, chief of the U.S. Army Air Corps, for May 28, 1940, in Washington, D.C.

The meeting did not go well; General Arnold was unable to be there. He sent General George H. Brett in his place. General Brett was late and had to leave early. He told Dr. Goddard to write a report on his proposals and send it to him. The junior officers present were not interested in rockets except for possible use to speed up planes. They told Goddard that he had not talked enough about his work; therefore, what funding for research on jet propulsion was available already had gone to the California Institute of Technology. In Goddard's opinion, research going on there was fifteen years behind his own.

Dr. Goddard wrote and sent his proposals to Washington within two weeks. While he waited for a reply, he wrote letters to Dr. Charles G. Abbot, to Senator David I. Walsh of Massachusetts, chairman of the Committee on Naval Affairs in the U.S. Senate, and to Clarence Hickman, his assistant during World War I. Clarence Hickman was now Dr. Hickman of Bell Telephone Laboratories, the large research facility of the American Telephone and Telegraph Company. Dr. Goddard told them what he had to offer his country as a result of his research. Unlike 1914, he had a working model, in fact, several of them. He protested that his work was far ahead of anyone else's, yet it was being overlooked.

Dr. Hickman was a true believer in Goddard's rocket. After all, he had sacrificed four of his fingers to it back in World War I. He believed government rocket research should be started immediately. Another idea he had was again to bring to the attention of the army the single-charge small rockets he had helped Goddard develop and demonstrate in the last days of World War I.

It was Dr. Hickman who was appointed by Dr. Bush to be chairman of Division A, the committee on powdered-propellant rockets for the National Defense Research Committee. Hickman arranged to have Dr. Goddard made, at least, a consultant to that division. But when Dr. Abbot of the Smithsonian heard about it, he was furious that Goddard had not been appointed to the committee for jet propulsion. He wrote a letter to Dr. Bush saying so.

In the middle of August 1940, Hickman asked Goddard to come to Washington, D.C., again. He stressed that it was so important for Goddard to be there immediately that Goddard took a plane. Once in Washington, Goddard made the rounds of admirals and generals, trying to interest them in funding rocket research for weapons. But General George H. Brett and the officers he had met with in May were gone, and his report was nowhere to be found in Washington. Goddard was sent to the Air Corps Research Center at Wright Field in Dayton, Ohio, where he was handed off from low-level official to low-level official who expressed little interest in his work.

Despite pleas from Hickman that he meet with one more admiral, Goddard packed up and went back to Roswell. He was exhausted and disgusted by the Washington runaround he had been given. He wrote to Dr. Atwood, president of Clark University:

> [T]he rocket is essentially a projectile which can be fired without recoil. Thus, with either powders or liquid fuel... it can be developed into a kind of very light and mobile artillery.... In addition, aviation engineers recognize that jet propulsion, or the use of rocket motors, will be necessary if we are to drive planes at much greater speeds, and at much higher altitudes, than are at present possible.

Goddard could not understand why he was being ignored.

When he had heard nothing further from Washington by the middle of September 1940, he fired off a letter to General Arnold asking for "a definite official decision... as to whether the Army Air Corps is interested in supporting this work." If the Army Air Corps wasn't interested, he would try the navy.

A few days later, he had his answer. The Army Air Corps was not interested in funding his research. If, however, he perfected a jet-assisted take-off device with Guggenheim Foundation funds, the Army Air Corps might be interested.

Getting government contracts for anything, whether it was manufacturing or research, required game playing, maneuvering, knowing the *right* people, and selling, selling, selling. Goddard wrote to Dr. Clarence Hickman, "If you can sell the idea of any part of the work, you would have my everlasting gratitude, for I have never had a talent for any kind of sales talk."

A few months later, the U.S. Navy put Dr. Hickman in charge of improving the recoilless gun Goddard and he had made in 1918. This weapon, using a powdered propellant, could blast its way through inches of armor plate. Hickman called it the *bazooka*. The bazooka was the reverse of a rocket in that all the burning of the fuel took place in the four-and-a-half-foot launch tube. Once out of the tube, the rocket coasted to its target. It could destroy a tank at close range. Yet one soldier could use it as easily as a rifle. Best of all, it only cost twenty dollars to make. This was the military's kind of weapon. Goddard was invited to work on the project for twenty dollars a day. He declined, but agreed that he could be called on as a consultant.

Besides Dr. Hickman, two young military engineers became acquainted with Goddard and were soon devoted disciples.

In the middle of 1940, Lieutenant Homer Boushey, an engineer and pilot in the Army Air Corps, wrote to Dr. Goddard about an invention of his own related to rocketry. He asked if he might come to Roswell to meet with him. Goddard, used to such requests, gave him the standard reply of drop by when in the neighborhood.

Boushey came, and the two men got on famously, for they found they shared many interests including H. G.

Wells's books. Goddard told Boushey more about his rocket than he had told anyone except his inner circle of Abbot, Atwood, Guggenheim, and Lindbergh. In return, Boushey was determined that he would do all he could to bring this wealth of knowledge Dr. Goddard had acquired over thirty years of study to the attention of the U.S. government.

Boushey was stationed at Wright Field in Dayton, Ohio. True to his word, Boushey did arouse the interest of his superiors. Somehow, Goddard's proposal originally sent to General Arnold was "found." But the Army Air Corps wanted to witness a static test of the power of Goddard's rocket engine. Goddard agreed, and the recently promoted Captain Boushey and two other men from the Army Air Force came to Roswell to see a test on July 11, 1941.

Of course, Nell did not work. Meanwhile, unable to resist the challenge, Goddard had drawn up a design and proposal for a jet-type take-off device. After all, he had been thinking about and experimenting with this concept since the early 1930s. He already held a patent on it. The patent for a "Propulsion Apparatus" was granted in 1934; in this apparatus, atmospheric air instead of liquid oxygen could be used in combustion.

A few days after the failed test, Boushey alone returned to witness another test. At last he saw the power of the rocket motors working. He wrote a report to his superior officers with high praise for the rocket.

Meanwhile, back at the ranch, Goddard had been contacted by Lieutenant Charles Fischer of the Navy Bureau of Aeronautics, whom he had met in 1939. Goddard sent the jet-type take-off device proposal to the U.S. Navy, too. After several months of study, the U.S. Navy proved faster than the Army Air Force in drawing up a contract for a year's work. Since government contracts were elusive, Goddard agreed to work for the U.S. Navy. There was a tie-in to the Army Air Force, but Goddard was truly sorry he would not be able to work with Boushey. The two thought so much alike, and Boushey had worked so hard on Goddard's behalf. Boushey was sent to work in California, with Dr. Theodor von Kármán, who also had a military contract for jet-assisted take-off devices.

Jet-assisted take-off devices, or jatos, were needed by the military so the distance required by a plane to take off could be shortened by up to 50 percent. At the same time, the plane could carry more weight. In the navy, it was needed so heavier planes like bombers could take off from aircraft carriers and land on small islands.

To fulfill the contract, Goddard had to hire more workers, double the size of his shop, and purchase more equipment. By December 3, 1941, he was running jato motor models in the testing stand successfully.

But in the development of these jet engines for planes, Goddard had something to worry about that he didn't have with Nell. He had to worry about the safety of the pilots who would fly the planes. There could be no combustion-tank explosions, no nozzles that burned through, no levers that stuck, causing the planes to crash. With this always in his mind, he devised controls the navy didn't even require. One of the most important was giving the pilot the ability to vary the power or turn it on and off during flight. In addition to being a safety device against engine malfunction, it allowed the pilot to give chase or make a getaway by giving his plane an extra burst of speed when he needed it.

Lieutenant Fischer oversaw the work at Roswell. When

Goddard sent in the report of his successful tests and, what is more, was ahead of schedule in his work, Lieutenant Fischer personally conducted the papers through the maze of naval bureaucracy. He made sure Goddard's work was brought to the attention of the admirals.

A few days after the successful test, the Japanese attacked Pearl Harbor, Hawaii. On December 8, the United States declared war on Japan. On December 11, Germany and Italy declared war on the United States.

Immediately, the U.S. government ordered every place doing government work to post an armed guard. For almost a month, Goddard and his assistants took turns staying up all night in the workshop until they could hire someone.

As Japan overran the Philippine Islands, Malaysia, Indonesia, and Burma within months, the U.S. war machine had to move into high gear. Early in 1942, Goddard was ordered to move his operation across the country from New Mexico to the Naval Engineering Experimental Station at Annapolis, Maryland, on the Severn River, where his rocket devices could be tested on seaplanes. He was to be director of research, Bureau of Aeronautics, Navy Department.

Dr. Goddard was happy to go because work on jatos had been going on at the experimental station for a year. He wrote, "It is the best news I have had for a long while. As I too feel that I can be of much more use working with those who are actually to apply the thrust unit." Goddard looked forward to working with other engineers and being in closer contact with Washington, where his work would be noticed and maybe bring him more contracts. But unknown to Goddard and almost everyone else, the U.S. government was pouring almost all its research money, over $2 billion, into a super weapon to end the war as quickly as possible—the atom bomb.

Esther Goddard was not happy over the move. They had just purchased Mescalero Ranch. She could see that her husband's health was failing even in the ideal climate of New Mexico because he was working too hard. She feared what the constant dampness of living near Chesapeake Bay would do to him.

The Goddards left Roswell by car for Annapolis on July 4, 1942, after packing up and shipping the equipment from the workshop and their furniture once again in a railroad freight car. They arrived in Annapolis on July 9. That same afternoon, Robert Goddard was put on an all-night train to Philadelphia, then went to New York and Providence, Rhode Island, as part of his work for the navy. He was a consultant on navy projects at installations in or near those cities. He had no sleep for two nights. By July 12, he was back in Annapolis planning his laboratory and workshop with the eight men who had come with him from Roswell.

Goddard found out what it was like to be in the mainstream of war work instead of ruling his own far-off domain. He was told that he and his men were expected to work seven days a week and there would be no vacations. Goddard refused to work his men seven days a week, although they never did get a vacation in four years. They had to punch time clocks, face inspections, and meet production deadlines. As Esther Goddard had feared, his health got worse. He had colds, constantly coughed, and was always tired. His hoarseness, which had started in New Mexico, was so bad that he talked in a whisper.

Goddard had to get a flight model of his motor ready for actual testing on a PBY. A PBY was an amphibious plane that could land or take off from water or land. It was used to rescue pilots, find enemy submarines, and carry cargo. It had two engines, and the wing went across the top of the plane with pontoons on the far ends of the wing. Goddard made engine after engine, each one giving more thrust power. The engine that he had tested in Roswell in December gave 300 pounds of thrust. By the end of August 1942, he could coax 1,200 pounds of thrust from his engines. Thrust of 1,000 to 3,000 pounds was needed for up to a minute to get heavier planes airborne from short runways.

In September, Lieutenant Fischer insisted that the engine was ready for flight testing. Goddard wanted more static tests. Over his objections, the engine was installed on a PBY. Lieutenant Fischer was to fly the jato-assisted plane himself. On September 23, the plane was loaded with sandbags to simulate the cargo it would usually carry. The test wasn't even tried with an empty plane first. Fischer had invited important naval officers to watch. Goddard and several men observed from a small crash rescue boat in the river. Goddard could tell by the shape and color of the flame coming out of the engine if everything was going as it should in the motor. If it wasn't, he was to warn Fischer in the cockpit of the plane by radio.

On the first test, the motor stopped in five seconds. A stainless steel sheet over the combustion chamber had heated up. Goddard ordered it removed. The second and third tests to measure take-off speed went well. But on the fourth test, when almost up to take-off speed, an igniter broke off. When it was fastened back on, a fifth test was tried, but the motor shut itself off again. The safety devices were working too well; they were removed.

On the sixth test, Fischer turned the jato engine on

full, and the big plane rushed through the waters of the Severn River faster and faster until it finally lifted off. Everyone cheered; Goddard worried.

Fischer landed the plane on the river, turned it into the wind, and went for another take-off. Seven was not his lucky number. Immediately, Goddard saw the flame was not right—too much oxygen. But when he tried the radio, it was jammed. He was helpless to warn his friend, and the plane took off. With the safety device removed that Goddard had built in because he foresaw this possibility, the liquid oxygen tank burst open and set fire to the tail of the plane burning the rudder. Although it was out of control, Fischer, a skilled pilot, managed to land the unwieldly plane in the water. Goddard and the men in the crash boat pulled him and his crew to safety.

After the PBY had been towed back to its hangar, Goddard's assistants took the rocket engine off and thoroughly examined it. Goddard angrily fired off recommendations to prevent such a near catastrophe from happening again. The first was, "1. A thermal cutoff device should be used at all times on the chamber.... No safety device on the chamber or unit should be removed before a run." But there never was another flight test of Goddard's engines. He was assigned to developing variable thrust engines that could have a force of 800 to 3,000 pounds that the pilot could control at will.

When Goddard wasn't working at his lab, he was traveling up and down the Atlantic coast to other factories and naval installations consulting on war work. Trains were crowded and never on time. Often he sat in cold railroad stations half the night. By June 1943, his wife persuaded him to see another tuberculosis specialist and a throat specialist in Baltimore. The TB specialist said what the others had said; he was amazed Goddard was alive. The throat specialist told him not to talk at all. That was impossible. He had to give instructions to his men. As each week passed, his assistants found him harder and harder to understand. Goddard tried writing out messages. He even resorted to tapping out messages in Morse code on his desk.

In August 1943, with great regret, he resigned from the faculty of Clark University. For nine years it had kept his place open for him as head of the physics department while he was in Roswell and then Annapolis. But Clark University had war work to do, too, and it needed someone permanently. Goddard knew he could not return to Clark to teach; he could not lecture with his failing voice. He also felt he was needed for the war work in Maryland. Besides, when the war was over, Harry Guggenheim, who was now a lieutenant commander in the navy, had promised to sponsor his rocket research again, so Goddard planned to return to Roswell.

Goddard had talked the navy into letting him design pumps like the ones he had developed in Roswell during the years from 1938 to 1941 to be used on the 300-pound thrust engine. But now the pumps would be ten times the size of the ones he had previously made. He convinced the navy that pumps would be much better than the old pressure flow they were using. He had discarded that method five years before.

Private industry began to take an interest in Goddard and jet propulsion. Soon after he arrived at Annapolis, the Curtiss-Wright Corporation contacted him about acting as a consultant to it on jet propulsion in postwar aviation. It also wanted the use of all Goddard's patents in return for royalty payments to him.

In addition to the Curtiss-Wright Corporation, the Linde Air Products Company, which had sold Goddard liquid oxygen for years, made him an offer similar to Curtiss-Wright's. It guaranteed him enough research funds to last ten to fifteen years. It was a complicated matter, and Harry Guggenheim sent Goddard to experienced lawyers in Washington, D.C., so that his interests and the interests of the Guggenheim Foundation would be preserved.

After several years of negotiations, an arrangement was worked out. Goddard's patents were protected as much as possible. He had a contract with the U.S. Navy to continue his work and a contract with Curtiss-Wright Corporation. He even worked as a part-time consultant on jet propulsion for the General Electric Company's laboratories in Schenectady, New York. They were working on the Whittle jet engine invented in England in 1939. It was to power a new plane made especially for jet engines by Bell Aircraft Company. The Bell XP-59 became the first American jet plane. By 1944, Goddard had ten patents or had applied for them on rocket operations and controls, twenty-two on combustion chambers, four on take-off and landing apparatus, and eight on gyroscopic steering. He had over thirty more besides, for a total of seventy-nine patents.

Other scientists could not understand Goddard's obsession with patents. But they had not been born and raised in Worcester, Massachusetts, where applying for patents was standard practice during the Industrial Revolution. It was a practice Nahum Goddard had taught his son.

During the war, any American who thought he had gotten to some place ahead of anyone else would scribble a sign saying, "Kilroy was here." In a letter to H. G. Wells,

Robert Goddard once wrote, "There can be no thought of finishing, for 'aiming at the stars,' both literally and figuratively, is a problem to occupy generations, so that no matter how much progress one makes, there is always the thrill of just beginning." Through his patents, anyone who would work on rocketry in the future would learn "Goddard was here."

Goddard, at last, joined the advisory board of the American Rocket Society. He consented to the society's republishing his 1919 extreme altitudes paper and his 1936 landmark paper, "Liquid Propellant Rocket Development." Any spare time he had, he spent organizing his papers.

No one knew Goddard's reason for establishing himself at last as the world's rocket pioneer. But it is a good thing he did.

10

The Trailblazer

By 1940, the Germans had swallowed most of Europe, although it gave them severe indigestion. England fought on alone, and Hitler was determined to have it, too. Mercilessly, he bombed England night after night from September on. Starting in 1942, England fought back with bomber raids on Germany. The English had the final revenge: the Allied D-Day invasion of France on June 6, 1944. But Germany was not through with England yet.

Less than a week after the Allied invasion, the Germans launched the V-1. The *V* stood for the first letter of the German word *vergetungswaffe* ("vengeance"). The V-1 was a light glider. It had a bullet-shaped head, a twenty-five-foot cylinder-shaped body made of metal, and squared off wings sixteen feet across. Inside the nose cone was a fuse set to go off on impact. That, in turn, ignited a ton of explosives. Before launching, its course was set and then maintained by a gyroscope. A shortwave radio sent back signals telling the Germans its flight path and where it landed. On top of the body over the tail and horizontal stabilizers was mounted a jet engine with a shutter-type intake. This made a buzzing sound in flight. But when the buzz stopped, it meant the bomb was about to hit its target, and the English people learned to run for bomb shelters. This "buzz bomb," as it was called, could travel a hundred miles. Its speed at launch was about 250 miles per hour. As it gained altitude, reaching as high as 5,000 feet, its speed increased to 450 miles per hour. Then its engines shut off, and it went into free flight, gliding into its target. Some 20,000 V-1s were launched against England before the Allies destroyed the launch sites on the coast of France near Calais and in Belgium.

When Goddard heard a detailed description of the V-1 bomb, he recognized at once that the idea was from the first pilotless guided missiles developed during World War 1 by Charles Kettering and Elmer Sperry. Sperry had perfected the automatic pilot for airplanes using a gyroscope. They installed the automatic pilots on propeller-driven aircraft loaded with bombs and preset the controls to get the plane to the target where it then dived at the target and exploded. As for the engine, Goddard recognized it as his own patented 1934 invention of a resonance motor using shutter-type valves. But the Germans had more surprises in store.

In September 1944, the Germans started using the largest object ever sent to the greatest heights by humans. It was the second vengeance weapon—the V-2 rocket—Hitler's *wunder-waffen,* the wonder weapon that Dr. Wernher von Braun and Dr. Walter Dornberger and thousands of scientists and engineers had been working on at Peenemünde since 1937.

The first one struck Paris; the second one London. The V-2 gave no warning, and its speed was so fast that there was no defense against it. The one-ton of explosives in the nose cone, or warhead, of the missile had terrible destructive powers. It could blast a hole thirty feet deep and thirty feet wide.

In March 1945, an unexploded V-2 was captured by the U.S. Army and sent to Dr. Goddard in Maryland for examination. When Goddard and his assistants removed the nose cone and the sleek cylindrical sides made of Duralumin, the suspicions he had had since World War I were confirmed. His work had been copied. The V-2 was Nell all grown up. It was forty-seven feet long, five feet in diameter, and weighed 9,000 pounds empty. It could carry 18,700 pounds of fuel—alcohol, water, and liquid oxygen—that provided 56,000 pounds of thrust. But the V-2 was not designed to go straight up as Goddard wanted his rocket to do. The one-half million horsepower of its engines pushed the rocket up over 60 miles into the atmosphere at speeds of 3,600 miles per hour. By then its fuel was used up. The engines shut off, and the V-2 arced over and glided toward its intended target up to 200 miles away from its launch site. But the Germans had pushed the V-2s into use before they had been perfected enough to be accurate in hitting their targets. A few missed England and hit neutral Sweden. Some 4,000 of them were launched by a desperate Germany.

While it had many times the power of Goddard's 1941 rockets, the V-2 was basically the same. He could see that all the parts were finely made out of the lightest materials,

The launching of a V-2 rocket from Peenemünde, the major Nazi missile research and testing center during World War II.

allowing for two-thirds of its weight to be fuel. The motor was made of carbon steel. Goddard counted at least six of his patents incorporated into the V-2.

The V-2 used liquid propellants and curtain cooling by spraying fuels through holes in the combustion chamber. The fuel pumps were driven by small turbines that used hydrogen peroxide instead of hot oxygen gas as God-

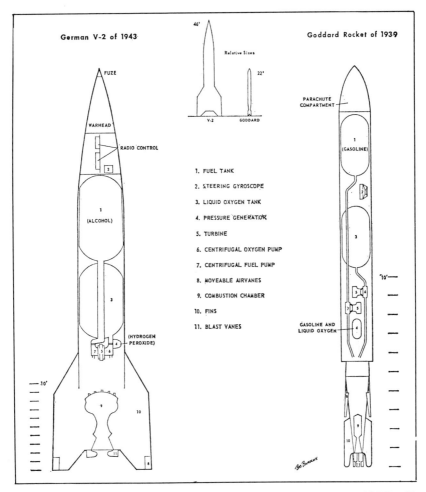

Diagram comparing the German V-2 rocket developed during World War II and Goddard's rocket of 1939.

dard's did—a small difference. Both the V-2 and Goddard's rocket were stabilized by gyroscopes and vanes at their backs. Even the parts of the V-2 were arranged in the same order inside as were those in Goddard's rocket.

There were two differences. In the nose cone of Goddard's rocket was a parachute. In the nose cone of the V-2 was a ton of explosives. One thing the V-2 had that Goddard's rocket did not have was a guidance system that allowed the V-2 to be set on a flight course before it left the launch site without further signals from the ground. This eliminated the need for in-flight radio direction, which could be jammed.

In May 1945, after Hitler died and Germany surrendered, Charles Lindbergh was asked by the U.S. government to visit the place where the V-2 rockets were made. He drove a jeep across the war-ravaged countryside to Nordhausen in the Harz Mountains of central Germany. There he found the V-2 factory—miles of tunnels had been dug deep into the solid rock of a mountainside safe from Allied bombs. It was like a coal mine complete with railroad tracks to move each V-2 missile around as it was being assembled. Eighteen thousand people had worked there before the factory was captured. Many of them were slave laborers from the infamous Bergen-Belsen concentration camp.

But now it was empty. Empty of slaves, empty of office workers, empty of scientists and engineers. They must have worked up until the moment of surrender, for Lindbergh found the lights had been left on.

Peenemünde had been captured by the Russians, and the Russians were to control Nordhausen, too, in what was to become East Germany. As soon as Hitler was dead, von Braun, Dornberger, and Hermann Oberth, with some 120 of the scientists and engineers who had worked on the V-2, bicycled their way to the American lines and surrendered. From Nordhausen itself, the U.S. Army removed 300 freight cars of V-2 parts and a ton of documents and plans. Some of these papers were frightening because they revealed that the Germans soon would have been capable of firing a rocket that could have hit New York City. When the

Germans were questioned by U.S. intelligence about the inner workings of the V-2 rockets, they looked at their interrogators in astonishment. Ask your own Dr. Goddard, they said. The U.S. intelligence officers had never heard of Goddard. Later, Wernher von Braun said, "Goddard was ahead of us all." He went on to say at other times that Goddard's work with liquid fuels saved the Germans years of work in perfecting the V-2.

With the capture of the V-2, the U.S. military was at last excited about high-altitude rockets. The U.S. Army launched studies. The Army Air Force had already asked Dr. Theodor von Kármán to write a long report on the possibilities of using missiles and satellites. The U.S. Navy did a study on space rocketry and awarded a research contract to the Guggenheim Aeronautical Laboratory at the California Institute of Technology. But all these studies of the V-2 papers, the V-2 itself, and future research were done in such tight security that no one knew what anyone else was working on. The army didn't know about the navy research; the navy didn't know about the air force's investigations.

Wernher von Braun began working on rockets in his spare time from his studies at school when he joined the Verein für Raumschiffahrt as a young teenager. He impressed then Captain Walter Dornberger, a brilliant scientist, who hired him as a civilian employee of the German army for rocket research at the age of twenty. Von Braun had studied under Hermann Oberth. Five years later von Braun was put in charge of a hundred men and all rocket research at Peenemünde where some twenty types of missiles were devised and tested out over the Baltic Sea. On October 3, 1942 by now General Dornberger and Dr. von Braun tested the V-2 rocket, but it was not ready to be put into use for two more years. Hitler put von Braun in prison for a while because he did not seem dedicated enough to Hitler's militaristic ambitions. Dornberger talked Hitler into releasing him by saying there would be no *wunder-waffen* without von Braun. With Peenemünde knocked out by Allied bombs and about to be overrun by the Russians, von Braun and his fellow scientists decided to surrender to the Americans. After he was brought to the United States, within a few months he was working for the United States at the White Sands Proving Ground in New Mexico. He showed the army how the V-2 worked and conducted experiments for it. White Sands was only a hundred miles as the rocket flies from Roswell.

For Robert Goddard there was nothing. He wrote to Colonel Homer Boushey,

> [T]here will be no consulting work on the American V-2. I think we can both understand where the brakes are being applied. . . . I am deeply grateful for your endeavor to have those in charge of Army affairs know about my work, but feel that anything started will sooner or later run against the same opposition.

Goddard continued his work for the navy. But he had to stay home more days. His voice was gone, and he had severe indigestion. On his first two-week vacation in four years, he spent most of his time sick in bed.

On June 2, Goddard once again went to Clark University, where he was awarded an honorary doctor of science degree.

Two weeks later, he had a severe choking spell. He visited a new doctor, who found a growth in his throat. Within two days, he was operated on at the University of

Maryland Hospital. The growth was found to be cancer, and his whole larynx had to be removed. He never left the hospital again. Dr. Robert Hutchings Goddard died on August 10, 1945.

Over the twenty-one years of their marriage, Esther Goddard had become as dedicated to the rocket as her husband was. With no children and in uncertain health, Robert Goddard often had told his wife that she was the only one who could carry on the work when he was gone.

Robert H. Goddard in a photograph taken a few months before his death in 1945. He is shown with a pump and generator developed for the U.S. military during World War II.

He even discouraged her flying lessons for fear something might happen to her.

Esther Goddard sold Mescalero Ranch. Before she left, she found two complete rockets in the workshop. In consultation with Harry Guggenheim, she sent them on a tour of museums across the United States before they were put on permanent exhibition at the Smithsonian Institution. On April 21, 1948, Esther Goddard stood with Guggenheim, Charles Lindbergh, and James Doolittle at the opening of the Goddard Rocket Exhibit at the American Museum of Natural History in New York City. Guggenheim and Lindbergh had also given their permission for Goddard's 1935 rocket, walled up for twelve years at the Smithsonian, to be put on display.

Esther Goddard moved back to Maple Hill in Worcester. She and three women she hired undertook the momentous task of organizing her husband's papers and photographs. On the advice of Harry Guggenheim and with the help of Dr. Goddard's longtime patent attorney, Charles T. Hawley, she applied for 131 more patents. The 214 Goddard patents held the key to rocketry. By 1951, it became apparent that the U.S. government was using many of them and not crediting Robert Goddard. The Guggenheim Foundation and Esther Goddard filed a joint claim against the government for infringement of Goddard's patents.

The army, navy, and air force each had its own space program to advance rocketry and develop a satellite to orbit Earth. This resulted in much duplication of effort and money wasted. In 1947, President Harry S Truman united all the military services under one Department of Defense. After that, the space and satellite programs were to be combined. However, all rocket development was limited to scientific study only. No money was available from Congress for new rocket weapons because Congress thought the country already had the ultimate weapon—the atom bomb. Delivery of the bomb already had been done satisfactorily by airplane. There was no need to develop missiles to deliver a bomb. It would be too expensive and have too little chance for success.

Then in 1950, the Korean War started. Suddenly, the military needed a rocket with a range up to 500 miles. Von Braun, Oberth, and their team were moved to the Redstone Arsenal at Huntsville, Alabama, and told to get busy designing a long-range military rocket.

While they worked on what was to become the Redstone rocket, the hydrogen bomb—much more powerful than the atom bomb—was successfully tested in 1952. The only problem was, in a few months, the Russians had one, too. The size of the hydrogen bomb was smaller than that of the atom bomb. When it was determined by mathematicians and scientists that a missile could carry it into space, work began on the intercontinental ballistic missile—the ICBM.

The Soviet Union was ahead of the United States in rocketry. After all, it had long experience with rockets, going all the way back to the ideas of Tsiolkovsky. During World War II it had used military rockets like the Katusha to drive the Germans from Stalingrad. It also had aircraft-launched rocket bombs weighing 230 pounds. Soviet leaders recognized rockets as proven offensive and defensive weapons. After World War II it speeded up research and development. On October 4, 1957, it launched the first orbiting satellite, *Sputnik,* which was about the size of a beach ball. This event electrified the world. After *Sputnik,* rockets were no longer the special domain of scientists and soldiers. *Sputnik* catapulted the people of the world into the space age.

As with the announcement of Goddard's attempt to build rockets to reach the moon back in 1920, there was overreaction to the Sputniks by the press and the public although many times greater. It was a great embarrassment to the United States not to be the first to put up a satellite, and it certainly was a propaganda victory for the Russians. The U.S. education system was criticized for not teaching enough math and science, and the U.S.S.R.'s system was extolled. The United States was said to lack science and technology skills and its industry was second-rate, leaving it so far behind the U.S.S.R. that it would never catch up. Gloom and doom was everywhere and lasted for years. But the United States was not behind.

On December 6 of that same year, the Americans attempted to launch a multistage Vanguard rocket. But it blew up on ignition. A few weeks later, the Russians did an even more spectacular launch. They put a 1,100-pound *Sputnik II* into orbit, and what is more, it carried a dog named Laika.

Finally on January 31, 1958, the United States succeeded in putting a satellite into orbit—*Explorer I. Explorer I* was developed under the direction of Dr. Wernher von Braun in cooperation with the California Institute of Technology's Jet Propulsion Laboratory. It did what Goddard had always hoped to do; it discovered unknown things in the atmosphere. At 594 miles up, *Explorer* ran into previously unknown heavy radiation. This became known as the Van Allen Radiation Belts after Dr. James A. Van Allen, who worked with Dr. von Braun on *Explorer I.*

With the race for space on, Congress created the National Aeronautics and Space Administration (NASA) in 1958. NASA took over and expanded the work of the National Advisory Committee for Aeronautics (NACA). All space efforts were coordinated under one agency. They were no longer fragmented between the army, the navy, the air force, universities, and private industry. The first NASA ten-year plan was laid before Congress in early 1960. It called for space flights with people on board, lunar and planetary probes, the photographing of the planets, and the development of larger rockets to send into space bigger, heavier payloads such as space stations. All this was estimated to cost over a billion dollars. After John F. Kennedy was elected president in 1960, he got behind NASA's ambitious plans by declaring, "I believe that this nation should commit itself to achieving the goal, before the decade is out, of landing a man on the moon and returning him safely to the earth."

NASA directed a coordinated effort to achieve that lofty goal. The first thing it did was build a new center for space science research, satellite development, flight operations, and tracking of orbiting satellites and space probes at Greenbelt, Maryland. On March 16, 1961, thirty-five years to the day after the first successful flight of a liquid-propellant rocket in Auburn, Massachusetts, the Robert H. Goddard Space Flight Center was dedicated.

At the dedication ceremonies, the Congressional Medal was presented to Esther Goddard for Dr. Goddard. On the back of the medal were the words from his high school graduation speech: "The Dream of Yesterday Is the Hope of Today and the Reality of Tomorrow."

Robert Goddard's research at last was recognized as the basis of all rocket work. Esther Goddard and the Daniel and Florence Guggenheim Foundation received a $1,000,000 settlement from the U.S. government for the right to use Goddard's patents. In accordance with the agreement Robert Goddard had signed thirty years before, the foundation received half of the settlement. Over the period of eleven years that the Guggenheim Foundation supported Goddard's work, it gave him over $180,000, an astonishing sum for the economically depressed 1930s. The Guggenheim Foundation used its share of the settlement to establish and fund Goddard professorships at Princeton University and the California Institute of Technology.

Robert Goddard designed, built, and launched thirty-five rockets. He developed the basic techniques that allowed rockets to fly. He was the first to (1) mathematically prove that rockets could reach extreme altitudes; (2) patent the idea of multistage rockets; (3) prove that a rocket can fly in a vacuum; (4) publish in the United States the theory and basic experiments of rocket propulsion and flight; (5) develop a successful motor using liquid propellants; (6) fly a liquid-propelled rocket; (7) use a gyrostabilizer and vanes to guide a rocket in flight; (8) launch a rocket that traveled faster than the speed of sound; (9) develop a modern rocket military projectile, which became the bazooka; (10) make pumps for rocket fuels; (11) develop curtain cooling for rocket combustion chambers; and (12) develop variable-thrust rocket motors.

Just as Robert Goddard outlined in his extreme altitudes paper of 1919, the exploration of Earth's atmosphere, the moon, and other planets has given humankind knowledge that could be gained no other way than by rockets. On July 20, 1969, American astronaut Neil Armstrong was the first man to walk on the surface of the moon seventy years after Robert Goddard's dream in the cherry tree.

Important Dates

1882 Robert Hutchings Goddard is born on October 5 in Worcester, Massachusetts, to Nahum and Fannie Hoyt Goddard.

1883 The Goddard family moves to Roxbury, Massachusetts.

1898 Robert Goddard reads H. G. Wells's *The War of the Worlds*.

1898 The Goddards move back to Worcester and live with Mary Goddard, Robert's grandmother.

1899 Robert Goddard has an idea for a space vehicle while sitting in a cherry tree on October 19.

1901–04 Goddard attends South High School in Worcester.

1904–08 Goddard studies electricity and physics at Worcester Polytechnic Institute.

1908–09 Goddard teaches at Worcester Polytechnic Institute.

1910 Goddard earns a master of arts degree from Clark University in electricity.

1911 Goddard earns a doctor of philosophy degree at Clark University.

1911–12 Goddard is an honorary fellow doing research at Clark University and presents a research paper to the American Physical Society at Harvard University.

1912–13 Goddard is a research instructor at Princeton University.

1913 Goddard becomes ill with tuberculosis.

1914 Goddard is made an instructor at Clark University.

1914 Goddard begins experiments with rockets.

1914 Goddard is granted two patents on ideas that become the Goddard rocket.

1915 Goddard is made an assistant professor at Clark University.

1917 The Smithsonian Institution begins support of Goddard's rocket research and continues its support through 1929 and in 1932.

1918 Goddard develops weapons for the U.S. Army during World War I including an early antitank weapon.

1919 Goddard's paper "A Method of Reaching Extreme Altitudes" is published by the Smithsonian Institution.

1920 Goddard is made a full professor of physics at Clark University.

1920–23 Goddard develops weapons for the U.S. Army at Indian Head, Maryland, in his spare time.

1923 Goddard is made head of the physics department at Clark University.

1924 Robert Goddard marries Esther Kisk on June 21 in Worcester, Massachusetts.

1926 Goddard develops a rocket propelled by liquid fuels that flies for the first time on March 16 at Auburn, Massachusetts.

1929 A fiery rocket flight on July 17 forces Goddard to move his tests from Auburn to the U.S. government's Camp Devens.

1929 Goddard meets Charles A. Lindbergh on November 23.

1930–32 Goddard works on rocket research in Roswell, New Mexico, with a $50,000 grant from the Daniel and Florence Guggenheim Foundation.

1932–34 Goddard teaches at Clark University, where he develops the forerunner of the jet engine for airplanes.

1934 Goddard returns to rocket research at Roswell sponsored by the Guggenheim Foundation, which continues to support his work through 1941.

1935 Goddard's rockets fly at the speed of sound.

1936 The Smithsonian Institution publishes Goddard's paper "Liquid-Propellant Rocket Development."

1938 Goddard's rocket reaches 6,565 feet on August 9, and the altitude is officially recorded by the National Aeronautics Association.

1941 Goddard makes last flights with rockets weighing 500 pounds and twenty-two feet long using turbine-power fuel pumps.

1941 Goddard begins development of jet-assisted take-off engines for the U.S. Navy.

1941 Japan attacks Pearl Harbor on December 7.

1942 Goddard is sent to Annapolis, Maryland, and appointed director of research, Bureau of Aeronautics, Navy Department.

1944 German V-1 and V-2 rockets launched.

1945 Goddard is given an honorary doctor of science degree by Clark University on June 2.

1945 Robert Goddard dies on August 10 in Baltimore, Maryland.

1956 The last of 214 patents is issued by the U.S. Patent Office in the name of Robert H. Goddard.

1960 The U.S. government makes a $1,000,000 settlement with Esther Goddard and the Guggenheim Foundation for the right to use Goddard patents.

1961 The Robert H. Goddard Space Flight Center is dedicated in Greenbelt, Maryland, on March 16.

1961 Robert H. Goddard is posthumously awarded the Congressional Medal of Honor on March 16.

1964 The Robert H. Goddard Commemorative Stamp is issued by the U.S. Post Office on October 5.

Places to Visit

Clark University. The Physics Department and the Robert H. Goddard Library contain collections of early rocket parts and photos.

National Air and Space Museum, Smithsonian Institution, Washington, D.C., contains four original Goddard rockets.

Roswell Museum and Planetarium, Roswell, New Mexico. In addition to parts of rockets, drawings, and photos, the launch tower and observation shed are on the grounds.

Worcester Polytechnic Institute, Worcester, Massachusetts, houses a collection of early rockets in Goddard Hall.

Goddard Tableau, Washington, D.C.

Robert H. Goddard Memorial Tower, Camp Devens, Massachusetts.

American Rocket Society Goddard Memorial at Auburn, Massachusetts, is the site of the first flight of a liquid-propellant rocket.

Bibliography

The Autobiography of Robert Hutchings Goddard: Father of the Space Age, Early Years to 1927. Worcester, Mass.: Achille J. St. Onge, 1966.

* Bilstein, Roger E. *Orders of Magnitude.* Washington, D.C.: NASA, 1989.

* Clark, Arthur C. *Man and Space.* New York: Time, 1964.

* Dewey, Anne Perkins. *Robert Goddard: Space Pioneer.* Boston: Little, Brown, 1962.

Goddard, Robert. *The Papers of Robert H. Goddard.* Edited by Esther G. Goddard. 3 vols. New York: McGraw-Hill, 1963.

Goddard, Robert H. "A Method of Reaching Extreme Altitudes." *Smithsonian Miscellaneous Collection*, Vol. 71, Publication 2656. Washington, D.C.: Smithsonian, 1920.

Kernan, Michael. "50th Anniversary of Step Toward Space." *Smithsonian Magazine* 6, 12 (1976): 77–80.

* Lehman, Milton. *The High Man: The Life of Robert H. Goddard.* New York: Farrar, Straus, 1963.

Lindbergh, Charles A. *Autobiography of Values.* New York: Harcourt Brace Jovanovich, 1976.

Mosley, Leonard. *Lindbergh: A Biography.* Garden City, N.Y.: Doubleday, 1976.

Pendray, G. Edward. *The Coming Age of Rocket Power.* New York: Harper and Brothers, 1945.

Shelton, William R. *Man's Conquest of Space.* Washington, D.C.: National Geographic, 1968.

Smith, LeRoi, ed. *We Came in Peace.* Chicago: Classic and Professional, 1969.

True, Webster P. *The First Hundred Years of the Smithsonian Institution, 1846–1946.* Washington, D.C.: Smithsonian, 1946.

* Wells, Herbert George. *The Complete Science Fiction Treasury of H. G. Wells.* New York: Avenell, 1978.

* Readers of Pioneer in Change's *Robert H. Goddard* will find this book particularly readable.

Index

About the Author

Karin Clafford Farley was born, raised, and still lives in the Chicago area. She earned bachelor's and master's degrees from the University of Illinois. Currently, she is a faculty member of the College of DuPage. Among previous books by the author is *Canal Boy*, a biography of James A. Garfield, twentieth president of the United States, and *Harry S. Truman, The Man from Independence*.

Author's Acknowledgments

I wish to thank Dorothy E. Mosakowski of the Robert Hutchings Goddard Library at Clark University in Worcester, Massachusetts, for photographs and permission to quote from Robert Goddard's writings and to Clark University and the McGraw-Hill Book Company for permission to use passages from *The Papers of Robert H. Goddard*, Vols. 1, 2, and 3, Esther K. Goddard and G. Edward Pendray, editors. I am indebted to the Chicago *Tribune* and the Worcester *Telegram and Gazette* for permission to quote headlines from their newspapers.

My thanks to NASA and the National Geographic Society for sending me informational material and to the Smithsonian Institution, which sent me literature and granted permission to quote from two Smithsonian publications: *A Method of Reaching Extreme Altitudes* by Robert H. Goddard and *The First Hundred Years of the Smithsonian Institution 1846–1946* by Webster P. True. The Smithsonian was the first to support financially and publish Robert Goddard's early research.

My appreciation to my husband, Jack, and to my daughter, Daryl, both electrical engineers, for their help with complex engineering and physics principles, proofreading, and all-round support. It has been a personally rewarding experience to research and write this book. My thanks to Richard G. Gallin, who suggested the idea for the book to me and edited the manuscript with enthusiasm and care.